T0303357

Praise for
The Lyric Essay as Resistance

"The view from the literary 'margins' has never looked as inspiring or as invigorating as it does in this collection of blazing bold voices that are pumping blood into the essay's very heart."
—**John D'Agata, author of** *About a Mountain*

"With Auden's elegy for Yeats, we tend to fixate on what poetry—or the lyric—*can't* do and forget that he goes on to say, 'it survives / In the valley of its making where executives / Would never want to tamper.' Indeed, its survival helps us better endure. This brilliant gathering of essayists that Bossiere and Trabold have curated for us is aimed square against kyriarchy. And the collection has me convinced. The lyric can be a powerful tool of resistance. Some truths can only be uttered from the margins."
—**Geoffrey Babbitt**

"This important and exciting anthology reveals how lyric essays can be both marginal and central, experimental yet sure, fluid and sound, haunted by ghosts but by beauty too. *The Lyric Essay as Resistance* is a gorgeous showcase of what the lyric essay can do."
—**Randon Billings Noble, editor of** *A Harp in the Stars:
An Anthology of Lyric Essays*

"I can easily see this fine anthology included in any of the courses I teach. The twenty essays herein do the triple-duty work of modeling the lyric form, expanding the platform for said form, and challenging the form to stretch so it can accommodate new, and necessary, literary voices."
—**Elena Passarello, author of** *Let Me Clear My Throat*
and *Animals Strike Curious Poses*

The

Lyric

Essay

as

Resistance

The Lyric Essay as Resistance

Truth from the Margins

Edited by
Zoë Bossiere and Erica Trabold

Wayne State University Press
Detroit

ISBN 978-0-8143-4960-1 (paperback)
ISBN 978-0-8143-4961-8 (e-book)

Library of Congress Control Number: 9780814349601

Wayne State University Press rests on Waawiyaataanong, also referred to as
Detroit, the ancestral and contemporary homeland of the Three Fires Confederacy.
These sovereign lands were granted by the Ojibwe, Odawa, Potawatomi, and
Wyandot Nations, in 1807, through the Treaty of Detroit. Wayne State University
Press affirms Indigenous sovereignty and honors all tribes with a connection to
Detroit. With our Native neighbors, the press works to advance educational equity
and promote a better future for the earth and all people.

*Grateful acknowledgment is made to the Leonard and Harriette Simons Endowed
Family Fund for the generous support of the publication of this volume.*

*Published with the assistance of a fund established by Thelma Gray James of Wayne State
University for the publication of folklore and English studies.*

Wayne State University Press
Leonard N. Simons Building
4809 Woodward Avenue
Detroit, Michigan 48201–1309

Visit us online at wsupress.wayne.edu

Contents

Introduction

nce, the lyric essay did not have a name.

Or, it was called by many names. More a quality of writing than a category, the form lived for centuries in the private *zuihitsu* journals of Japanese court ladies, the melodic folktales told by marketplace troubadours, and the subversive prose poems penned by the European romantics.

·

Before I came to lyric essays, I came to writing. When my teacher asked the class to write a story *for homework*, I couldn't believe my luck. But in response to my first attempt, she wrote in the margins: *this is cliché.*

As a first-generation college student, I was afraid I didn't know how to tell a story properly, that my mind didn't work that way. That I didn't belong in a college classroom, wasn't a real writer.

And yet, language pulled me. Alone in my dorm room, I arranged and rearranged words, whispered them aloud until the cadences pleased me, their smooth sounds like prayers. I had no name for what I was writing then, but it felt like a style I could call my own.

—Erica

•

While the origins of the lyric essay predate its naming, the most well-known attempt to categorize the form came in 1997, when writers John D'Agata and Deborah Tall, coeditors of *Seneca Review*, noticed a "new" genre in the submission queue—not quite poetry, but neither quite narrative.

This form-between-forms seemed to ignore the conventions of prose writing—such as a linear chronology, narrative, and plot—in favor of embracing more liminal styles, moving by association rather than story, dancing around unspoken truths, devolving into a swirling series of digressions.

D'Agata and Tall's proposed term for this kind of writing, "the lyric essay," stuck, and in the ensuing decade the phrase would be adopted by many essayists to describe the kind of writing they do.

•

As a genderfluid writer and as a writing teacher, I've always appreciated the lyric essay as a literary beacon amid turbulent narrative waves. A means to cast light on negative space, to illuminate subjects that defy the conventions of traditional essay writing.

Introducing this writing style to students is among my favorite course units. Semester after semester, the students most drawn to the lyric essay tend to be those who enter the classroom from the margins, whose perspectives are least likely to be included on course reading lists.

—Zoë

.

Since its naming, the lyric essay has existed in an almost paradoxical space, at once celebrated for its unique characteristics while also relegated to the margins of creative nonfiction. Perhaps because of this contradiction, much of the conversation about the lyric essay—the definition of what it is and does, where it fits on the spectrum of nonfiction and poetry, whether it has a place in literary journals and in the creative writing classroom—remains unsettled, extending into the present.

.

I thought getting accepted into a graduate program meant I had finally opened the gilded, solid oak doors of academia—a place no one in my family, not a parent, an aunt or uncle, a sibling or cousin, had ever seen the other side of.

But at my cohort's first meeting in a state a thousand miles from home, I understood I was still on the outside of something.

"Are you *sure* you write lyric essays?" the other writers asked. "What does that even mean?"

—Erica

•

The acceptance of the lyric form seems to depend largely on who is writing it. The essays that tend to thrive in dominant-culture spaces like academia and publishing are often written by writers who already occupy those spaces. This may be part of why, despite its expansive nature, many of the most widely anthologized, widely read, and widely taught lyric essays represent a narrow range of perspectives: most often, those of the center.

•

To name the lyric essay—to name anything—is to construct rules about what an essay called "lyric" should look like on the page, should examine in its prose, even whom it should be written by. But this categorization has its uses, too.

Much like when a person openly identifies as *queer*, identifying an essayistic style as "lyric" provides a blueprint for others on the margins to name their experiences—a form through which to speak their truths.

—Zoë

•

The center is, by definition, a limited perspective, capable of viewing only itself.

In "Marginality as a Site of Resistance," bell hooks positions the margins not as a state "one wishes to lose, to give up, or surrender as part of moving into the center, but rather as a site one stays on, clings to even, because it nourishes one's capacity to resist."

To write from the margins is to write from the perspective of the whole—to see the world from both the margins and the center.

·

I graduated with a manuscript of lyric essays, one that coalesced into my first book. That book went on to win a prize judged by John D'Agata and named for Deborah Tall. I had finally found my footing, unlocked that proverbial door. But skepticism followed me in.

On my book tour, I was invited to read at my alma mater alongside another writer whose nonfiction tackled pressing social issues with urgency, empathy, and wit. I read an essay about home and friendship, about being young and the hard lessons of growing up.

After the reading, we fielded a Q&A. The dean of my former college raised his hand.

"I can see what work the other writer is doing quite clearly," he said to me. "But what exactly is the point of yours?"

—Erica

·

Writing is never a neutral act. Although a rallying slogan from a different era and cause, the maxim "the personal is political" still applies to the important work writers do when they speak truth to power, call attention to injustice, and advocate for social change.

Because the lyric essay is fluid, able to occupy both marginal and center spaces, it is a form uniquely suited to telling stories on the writer's terms, without losing sight of where the writer comes from and the audiences they are writing toward.

When we tell the stories of our lives—especially when those stories challenge assumptions about who we are—it is an act of resistance.

.

Many of the contemporary LGBTQIA+ essayists I teach in my classes write lyrical prose to capture queer experience on the page. Their works reckon with nonbinary family building and parenthood, the ghosts of trans Midwestern origin, coming of age in a queer Black body, the overwhelming epidemic of transmisogyny and gendered violence.

The lyric essay is an ideal container for these stories, each a unique prism reflecting the ambiguous, messy, and ever-evolving processes through which we as queer people come to understand ourselves.

—Zoë

.

Lyric essays rarely stop to provide directions, instead mapping the reader on a journey into the writer's world, toward an unknown end. Along the way, the reader learns to interpret the signs, begins to understand that the roadblocks and potholes and detours—those gaps, the words left unspoken on the page—are as important as the essay's destination.

•

The lyric essays that have taught me the most as a writer never showed their full hand. Each became its own puzzle, with secrets to unlock. When the text on a page was obscured, the essay taught me to fill in the blanks. When the conflict didn't resolve, I realized irresolution might be its truest end. When the segments of the essay seemed unconnected, I learned to read between the lines.

The most powerful lyric essays reclaim silence from the silencers, becoming a space of agency for writers whose experiences are routinely questioned, flattened, or appropriated.

Readers from the margins, those who have themselves been silenced, recognize the game.

—Erica

•

The twenty contemporary lyric essays in this volume embody resistance through content, style, design, and form, representing a broad spectrum of experiences that illustrate how identities can intersect, conflict, and even resist one another. Together, they provide a dynamic example of the lyric essay's range of expression while showcasing some of the most visionary contemporary essayists writing in the form today.

These stories are complex, and don't always have tidy or happy endings. The experiences they depict may not be immediately relatable or accessible to every reader. But our hope for *The Lyric Essay as Resistance: Truth from the Margins* is for every voice to speak without compromise. To nourish the capacity for a new generation of lyric essayists to take up the important work of resistance.

Apocalypse Logic

Elissa Washuta

y great-great-great-grandfather Tumalth, headman of the Cascades, was hanged by the U.S. Army in 1856, a year after signing the Kalapuya Treaty. He was accused of treason, but he was innocent. I feel like I should say I'm tired of writing this again. I am always writing that Tumalth was hanged a year after signing the Kalapuya Treaty. I am always writing that his daughters were taken to Fort Vancouver when the Cascade leaders were hanged. I am always writing about the resistance of the women who hung tough along the Columbia River for generations, even after the disruption of the systems of hunting, fishing, and gathering our family maintained for thousands of years. Actually, I'm not tired of writing about this, and I may never be, but sometimes when I say once more that *my great-great-great-grandfather was hanged by the U.S. government* I can feel someone thinking, *God, she's back on that.*

The last time I watched television, a man kept touching a screen with a red-and-blue map on it. After a while, I was nauseous and my whole body felt held up by metal rods. *Stop putting your hands on that map,* I wanted to tell him. I was in a huge room full of people who were booing, crying, and drinking heavily. *Termination,* I thought. *They are going to terminate my tribe. They are going to finish what they started.* I am certain that I was the only person in the whole venue—a concert space—thinking about tribal termination. I am always in this room and I am always lonely.

X

From 1953 to 1968, the U.S. government tried to wipe out some tribes by ending their relationships—withdrawing federal recognition of these tribes as sovereigns, ending the federal trust responsibility to those tribes, allowing land to be lost to non-Natives. The tribes terminated, for the most part, were those the U.S. government considered to be successful because of the wealth within their tribal lands: timber, oil, water, and so on. Terminating a tribe meant fully forsaking all treaty responsibilities to them.

X

In 1993, Donald Trump testified in front of the House Native American Affairs Subcommittee:

If you look, if you look at some of the reservations that you've approved, that you, sir, in your great wisdom have approved, I will tell you right now—they don't look like Indians to me. And they don't look like the Indians. . . . Now, maybe we say politically correct or not politically correct, they don't look like Indians to me, and they don't look like Indians to Indians.

Earlier that year, Trump had made efforts to partner with the Agua Caliente Band of the Cahuilla Indians as manager of their proposed casino near Palm Springs. The tribe declined.

In 2000, Donald Trump sent a gold-monogrammed letter to the Cowlitz Indian Tribe, of which I am an enrolled member. Hoping to partner with us, he toured our proposed casino site, which he said was the most incredible site he'd ever seen. In 2002, Trump submitted a proposal to partner with the tribe in developing the casino. The tribe declined.

In the letter he sent us in 2000, he wrote, "I want to assure you and all of the members of the Tribe that I do now, and always have, supported the sovereignty of Native Americans and their right to pursue all lawful opportunities."

Our casino will open in April. By then, Donald Trump will have a hand in determining what's lawful.

X

While I watched television and listened to the pundits talk about the man who loves revenge, I began having a panic attack that, as I write this, is eight days deep, the longest I can remember in my decade of PTSD, which I developed and cultivated as a response to multiple rapes, sexual assaults, threats of violence, and acts of stalking that accumulated over the years. For me, a panic attack is dread made physical, an embodied trauma response: nausea, insomnia, a pounding heart, headaches. My psychiatrist said my triggers are many because I went years without PTSD treatment.

In *The Beginning and End of Rape*, Sarah Deer writes, "Colonization and colonizing institutions use tactics that are no different from those of sexual perpetrators, including deceit, manipulation, humiliation, and physical force."

I watched the man touch his hand to the map and knew what my body was trying to tell me: the sexual violence against my body has been carried out in response to the settler state's instructions to its white men, and now the instructions would be delivered clearly, from behind no screen. Maybe my triggers are many because to live in the United States of America is to wake up every day inside an abuser.

X

Boston is the chinuk wawa word for *white* (adj.) or *white person* (n.).

Boston-tilixam also means *white person*, or *white people*.

Siwash is the white people word for *savage Indian* (n.).

I saw the word *siwash* attached to a photo embedded in a wall in a park in the Seattle suburbs.

I know only a few words in chinuk wawa:

Mahsie is thank you.
Klahowya is hello.

Some people say chinuk wawa, also known as Chinook jargon, isn't a real language. This, I think, is because, before the boston-tilixam had us speak English, the jargon was the assemblage of words we used to talk to each other, all up and down the coast.

X

A few days after the last time I watched television, I went to a community response forum in my neighborhood. A line of people hugged the side of the building, waiting to enter. Two boston-tilixam asked the people in line behind me, "Is this the line to get in?" When they heard that it was, they went to the front of the line. Inside, a volunteer said that people who live north of the ship canal would meet in a gallery down the block; people south of the ship canal would stay here and would split into groups by neighborhood. A group of boston-tilixam didn't want to be split up. The volunteer assured them that it wasn't *mandatory* that they separate. The boston-tilixam, relieved, chose a group they could all agree upon.

X

Chief Tumalth's daughter Virginia Miller (my great-great-grand-mother's sister) was photographed by Edward Curtis, a boston best known for his sepia-toned portraits of unsmiling Indians posed in their ceremonial dress. Curtis interviewed Virginia, who spoke through an interpreter about traditional Cascade life and her father's hanging. And she told Curtis this, presented here in his words:

> An old man dreamed and announced that new people were com-ing, with new ways, and the Indians would die. He made them put coyote-skins over their shoulders and two by two, men in front and women behind, march in a circle, while he sang his song of prophecy. The old woman who told [Virginia] about this said it happened when she was a little girl. She took part in the dance, and laughed at the flapping tail of the skin on the girl in front of her, and the old man seized her by the wrist, flung her aside and said, "You will be the first to die." As it happened, she outlived all the others.

X

The U.S. has been a party to many treaties.

Some bind the U.S. to its allies: an armed attack on one member of the alliance is considered a threat to the other members, who agree to "act to meet the common danger."

Some are with other international sovereigns, settling all sorts of agreements.

Some are with tribes; all of these have been broken.

One is with my great-great-great-grandfather and a bunch of other men, some of whom were hanged for treason.

The U.S. did not enter into treaties with tribes in order to create alliances.

This feels like a logic game that I am too tired to play.

X

Now I see I'm inclined to write, again, about how my great-grandma gave birth to my grandmother with no help but from scissors and string because she didn't want any boston woman messing with her. Like I do in all my essays, I try to explain that she did this at a time when boston-tilixam were stealing Indian babies because it was the quickest and easiest way to turn Native people into boston-tilixam: turn their tongues before they take on an Indigenous language they'll have to unlearn, keep them sheared so there will be no braids to cut. I am alive because of the scissors and the string, because of the everyday resistance that led my great-grandmother to turn away the boston ladies who wanted to help her learn to do white lady things like crochet.

I am most thoroughly colonized by the desire to have the boston-tilixam like me. I look like them, and I try to use this to say things that wouldn't be tolerated from someone who doesn't look like them. But sometimes my desire silences me. Sometimes it speaks so loudly that I can hardly hear the ancestors' instructions for surviving genocide.

X

I sleep less than before. I wake up before sunrise and research things I don't understand. The river where Edward Curtis photographed Virginia Miller with her canoe, the river that is home to salmon and smelt and steelhead, the river where my family lived for ten thousand years—I am forced to imagine it covered in oil. I learned about Environmental Impact Statements and tribal consultation ten years ago, when I was in an entry-level position with the USDA Natural Resources Conservation Service, making best practices flowcharts and compiling resource manuals, but I abandoned that to become a writer.

Boston-tilixam keep asking me, "What can we do?" and I explain that the Lower Columbia River Estuary—our tribal homeland—is threatened by a proposed oil terminal, methanol plant, and coal terminal that could bring major environmental disaster and undermine ongoing habitat restoration efforts. The Army Corps of Engineers is ignoring tribes' concerns despite active tribal involvement in the consultation process. The coal terminal's environmental impact statement says, "As it currently stands, the tribes exercise their treaty fishing rights in Zone 6, which is outside of the NEPA scope of analysis for this EIS." The focus here is narrow and fails to respond to concerns about coal train dust. This would be the largest coal export terminal in North America.

I tell my Facebook friends that the public comment period is still open. I wonder whether there will be a point at which direct action like the water protection at Standing Rock would be needed, but it's too early to know.

I am wedged inside a small window in the boston people's attention, and I am screaming.

X

In James Welch's novel *Winter in the Blood*, white men gather in a bar alongside the Native American narrator. "But you're mistaken—there aren't any goldeyes in this river. I've never even heard of goldeyes," one of the white men tells the (unnamed) narrator. Another one says, "There are pike in the reservoir south of town. Just the other day I caught a nice bunch." They continue to disagree. The narrator asks, "In the reservoir?"

I want to know whether he thinks there are fish in the river, or in the reservoir, or anywhere, but instead he studies the white men in suits and listens to them talk about the sunfish and the goldeyes and the "clarity of the water" until the subject changes.

X

In 1957, Celilo Falls, part of the Columbia River near where my family is from, was the oldest continuously inhabited community in North America, with archaeological records dating Celilo village sites to 11,000 years ago. This was once an important site for trade and fisheries, but the opening of the Dalles Dam created a reservoir that flooded Celilo Falls and Celilo Village to make Lake Celilo. Last year, the Army Corps of Engineers thought it might be neat to lower the water for a couple of weeks to reveal Celilo Falls again. Susan Guerin (Warm

Springs) wrote of the idea, "My people can't return to Celilo Falls to fish. It won't mend the broken hearts of my family from whom the Celilo Falls were taken. The study will tear off wounds long scabbed-over, and for what; the benefit of spectators?"

X

I used to like to keep safety pins attached to my messenger bag because I used them to clean pepper out of my teeth when I was out of the house.

I used to drink water straight from the tap.

I used to have no idea what my blood quantum was because nobody had ever thought to tell me something like that.

I began to carry floss.

I began to drink from cups.

I began to tell people my blood quantum when they asked, even when I didn't want to.

Somewhere, someone wearing a safety pin on her jacket is saying to someone else, I'm so sorry for what your ancestors went through. May I ask, are you full Native?

X

Boston man: white man.

Boston klootchman: white woman.

Many white fur traders, the first whites to occupy the Lower

Columbia River Plateau, were from the city of Boston.

Boston Illahee: The United States of America.

I am the descendant of Chief Tumalth of the Cascade people. The United States in which I live is the descendant of the Boston Illahee in which Tumalth was hanged under orders of Philip Sheridan—"The only good Indians I ever saw were dead"—and his daughters were taken by the military to Fort Vancouver.

Why I have used boston in this essay when I am talking about white people: for the white people who have already made up their minds about their own whiteness; for the white people who have forgotten that their whiteness is new here, that whiteness is not a phenotype but a way of relating; for the white people who don't believe me when I say that the most thorough answer to the question, "What can we do?" is, "Remove your settler state from this land and restore all governance to its forever stewards."

X

At the end of *Dances with Wolves*, Wind in His Hair shouts down to Lt. Dunbar from a cliff. The English subtitles read, "Do you see that you are my friend? Can you see that you will always be my friend?"

Because I don't want boston-tilixam to think I am a *nasty woman*—there is already a word for this when applied to Native women, a word we don't use, which is *squaw*—I want to explain that I love many boston-tilixam. Some are relatives; some I love so much that they are family to me; this has nothing to do with anything and I'm embarrassed that

I even feel the need to say it. There are some boston-tilixam I don't like, but it's not because of their whiteness. Sometimes, it is about the things their whiteness motivates them to say and do, but none of that is really my business. The boston-tilixam are responsible for their own whiteness.

When the boston-tilixam came here, we traded at the river.

When they wanted our land, representatives of Boston Illahee killed and relocated us.

I am descended from many boston-tilixam and I hold them inside my Indigenous body. I look like them. I have never said that I "walk in two worlds." I walk in the world in which Native nations welcomed visitors who responded by creating a government on our forever land whose mistreatment benefits them.

I don't know of a chinuk wawa word that translates exactly to *whiteness*, maybe because we experience it not as an abstract noun but as an action verb. None of us can choose the legacy we are born within, but all of us choose our alliances. We make and reinforce our commitments with every action.

The problem: that Indigeneity is viewed by the boston-tilixam as a burden while whiteness is not.

The result: some boston-tilixam pour energy into defending the wearing of safety pins.

The weather forecast for Standing Rock: blizzards.

X

"You're an old-timer," the narrator of *Winter in the Blood* says to a man he meets in a café. "Have you ever known this river to have fish in it?" The old man only says "Heh, heh," before he drops dead, facedown into his oatmeal.

My students, at times, used to struggle with the fish motif. Maybe that happened because I couldn't guide them through seeing the river as symbol. How can we speak in metaphor when we need the river to be seen as literal?

X

For a while, I thought that, because my work had me at energetic, physical, and emotional capacity, I was doing enough. I was writing, teaching, and informally educating. I changed my mind last week. I found more energy; it had been tucked into night hours I used to use for sleeping. I want to rest, to comfort myself, to meditate, to relax, to practice self-care, but I have a sick belly and a sunken face now. I would like to take a break from the work, but my nausea is telling me that I don't really have a choice. I can't let myself stop with small steps—a Facebook post, a retweet—when Native people are being tear gassed, shot with rubber bullets, and threatened with live ammunition for doing the thing the ancestors are still, from within my body, from the other side of genocide, doing: committing to the river.

I want to hold the scissors. I want to tie tight, constricting knots with the string. I want to inhabit my body so fully that I know how to use it to protect the people and the land I love. Because I, too,

21

am asking, *How can I help? What can I do?* And my ancestors tell me clearly, *Find us in your body and we will show you.*

X

When the Cascade leaders were hanged, some of the people went onto reservations and some remained in the homelands by the river. These people, like my family, were called renegades. To be a renegade is to have betrayed an alliance. Who is betrayed by the act of staying alive in the place where one has lived for ten thousand years?

Tumalth signed that treaty with his X that meant he and his fellows would *acknowledge their dependence on the government of the United States, and promise to be friendly with all the citizens thereof, and pledge themselves to commit no depredations on the property of such citizens.*

If my survival is a betrayal, make no mistake: I'll betray.

X

Tyee is chief. *Tumtum* is heart. *Klushkakwa* is not a word I can translate for you but you might hear me say it instead of *goodbye*, which is not what it means. Instead of *goodbye*, my mom says *toodle-oo* because saying goodbye isn't done, just like stirring batter counterclockwise, just like walking on the parts of the cemetery where there are graves that could cave in. If this doesn't make sense, don't think about it. Don't try to find explanations consistent with what might be called *logic*. Know that, if you are not from a post-apocalyptic people, you may not be familiar with these strategies we use to survive.

If you are a boston and when you hear me mention that my tribe's casino will open in April your first impulse is to say it's a shame that we're doing that, try this instead: trust that we are doing what we believe will help us survive your nation. Instead, say it's a shame that we are still forced to react to the settler state built upon intentional efforts to kill us all.

X

During the summer of 1829, four-fifths of the Cascade people were killed by a white disease. The year before Tumalth signed the treaty, there were only eighty Cascade people left.

Apocalypse comes from an ancient Greek word that's supposed to mean *through the concealed.*

Apocalypse has very little to do with the end of the world and every-thing to do with vision that sees the hidden, that dismantles the screen.

We have known for a long time that they intend to kill us. I have spent almost every moment of my life in an America that will not rest until I am either dead or turned boston klootchman. I make my way in an America that wants to assign me whiteness because that will mean they've exterminated the siwash they see in me.

It doesn't work that way and it never has.

Boston-tilixam ask me, *What can I do?* And I talk about the river. Klushkakwa.

23

A Meditation on Grief: Things We Carry, Things We Remember

Crystal Wilkinson

remember this place where burdens wash away in the dark and mothers' dresses float like blossoms, a boy drowns—his head turned toward home—body facing the farmer's house, where the girl who loves him sleeps. She is the farmer's daughter. They say she is the one who hit his head, the one who hoisted the rock, the one who watched his blood ooze out. *This is the way you wash your clothes in the creek. This is the way you catch catfish in deep water.* The mothers stand in water to their knees, their dresses wafting out like sheets on a line. On the creek bank, a child runs circles catching the wind and the mothers' dresses float like blossoms. The mothers sing prayers for the boy's mother who looks out her kitchen window and cries. The circle of mothers in the water whispers a prayer for the girl who tells all who will listen that she loved the boy who died. Her mother stands in the backyard, her hand on the chopping hoe with tears streaming down her face. The fathers brood in the fields, walking slow as lepers, hearts and houses filled with grief.

I almost drowned once, my grandmother's dress blossomed around her like a sail. She was my johnboat in the creek. My mother stood on the shore frozen with fear, my father's name mute on her tongue, his kiss spoiled fruit in her young sweet mouth. That dead boy's ghost haunts this place, dark water flowing like a deacon's robe. On nights spoiled with teenage trouble, I went to the creek and waited for the boy, hoping he would listen. *Do you dream of the farmer's daughter?* I asked. *Are you sorry for what you've done?* He didn't answer. They say he raped the girl but I wasn't afraid of him. By then I had been raped, too, and was becoming a dangerous woman. I waited for him and held court with the moon. *I'm here,* I said. *Let's get this done!* In this place where burdens washed away I stood, my dress flowering, floating. I was drowning too—my face turned toward home—my black body facing my father's house, where my mother cried for me. They say the boy was handsome, but I never saw him in the flesh. At night the creek did scare me, its rush like a boy's whispered threat in a girl's ear. But here the mothers are always standing with water to their knees, their dresses billowing out like sheets on a line, praying because there was always something roaring in those trees, teeth gnashing, fathers killing boys for the sake of their daughters, eyes always watching, eyes always glistening in the dark.

The Story You Never Tell

Chelsea Biondolillo

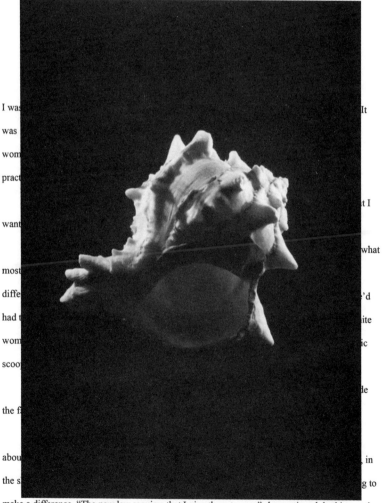

I was It

was

wom

prac

want t I

most what

diffe 'd

had t ite

wom ic

scoo

le

the f

abou , in

the s g to

make a difference. "The new law requires that I give these to you," she continued, looking each of us in the eye, trying to connect, "but the law cannot make you open it."

docu...   ...ated

by m...

...and

babi...

deve...   ...f the

cellu...

durin...   ...r

hand...

...lf.

...vers

in th...   ...sea

of br...

...I

will ...   ...ck to

look...

chec...   ...ed

to do...

I understood that I had gotten myself into trouble, and had to pay to get out of it. There had neve r been any question for me about what was going to happen when that extra pink stripe

show   a

giant   ts.

So, r   to

be al $60

for tl

year   my

$4.8

                                                                                             of

myse   let.

                                                                                             n a

lava   ent.

Plus

hopi

pictu   be

disce

wom   linic

recep   e.

Wha

And

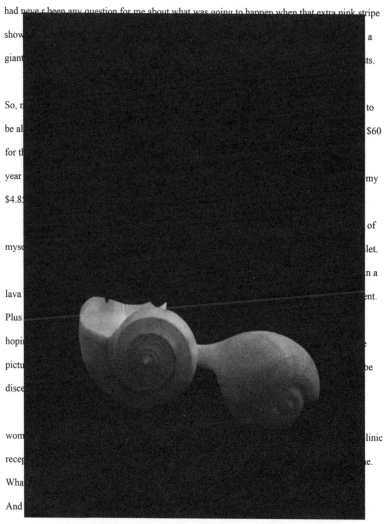

I remember counting backwards as the shot took effect. I remember the counselor holding

my hand and asking me what my major in college had been. I remember a sharp pain, my free
hand   ll
like,
woul
wom
                                                                                         g
the d

I no
alwa
susp   Abita
beer

John
kind

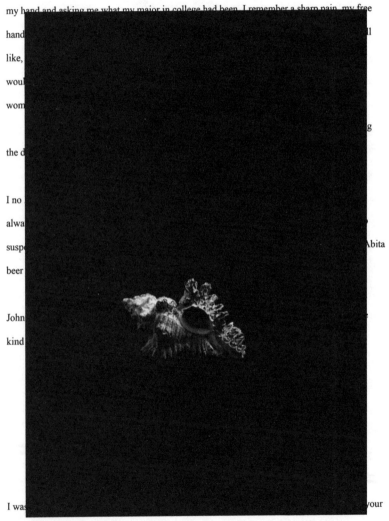

I wa   your
doorstep would mean. "Gilded Splinters" is basically a spell to bring voodoo vengeance down on

Dr. John's unnamed enemies. A long, wailing, trippy curse. New Orleans is a superstitious town.

It's e

Whe

stree   rs is

a tatt

anytl

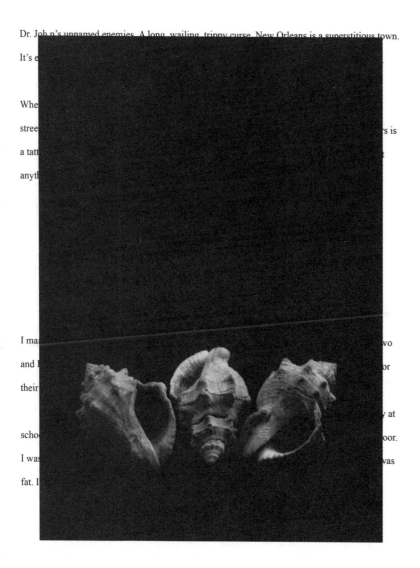

I ma   wo

and I   or

their

                                                                          y at

scho   oor.

I was   vas

fat. I

I had

seve

But t

happ   e of

those

                                                                         my

poor   word

for t   ..

well,   no

was   re

like   ave

been

I've had this conversation in my head so many times, because it's not a conversation that's easy to have out loud. It's a story that makes people uncomfortable.

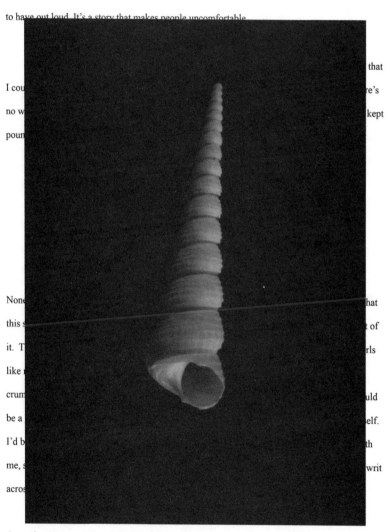

that
I cou   re's
no w   kept
poun

None   hat
this s   t of
it. T   rls
like   crum   uld
be a   elf.
I'd b   th
me, s   writ
acros

Around.

Before the man who'd pulled off my jeans and then my tights, there was the man who got

me s no

whe

beau

okay say

no, s

wait

okay

en I

tried

actin

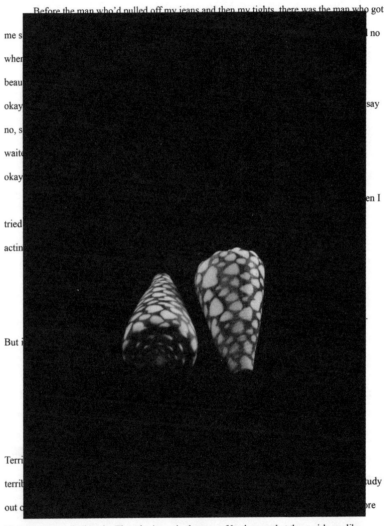

But

Terri

terrib udy

out re

likely to be assaulted again. They don't say in the paper, You know what those girls are like, because everyone knows. It's just math

med.

I nev

Whe   rs, I

thou

panty

unde   g for

troub

As w

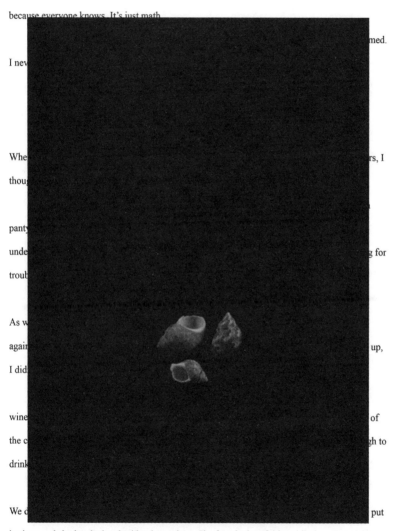

agai   up,

I did

wine   of

the c   gh to

drink

We   put

back on and she laughed and said to leave them. She found a lot of things hilarious that night.

She hadn't gone through with it, of course. Just me. Because out in the trees alone with him

push   and

my t   uld I

know

                                                                         ow

much   . She

was   ing

but h

                                                                       ick

smu

                                                                      hed

dark   ld

neve   at

the s

                                                                    ould

final   ly in

the s   n,

for s   s

slick

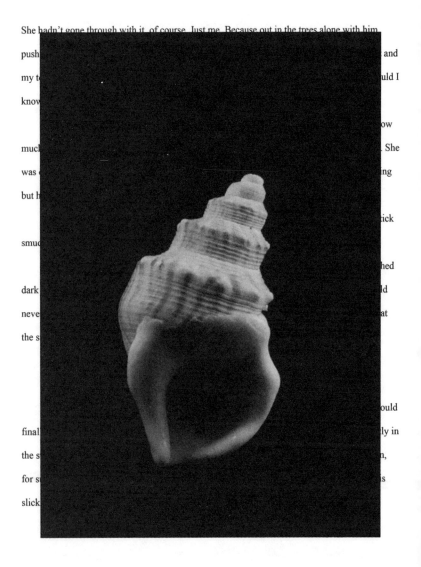

Roll outta my coffin

I wo

Once

appr   n

me g   let

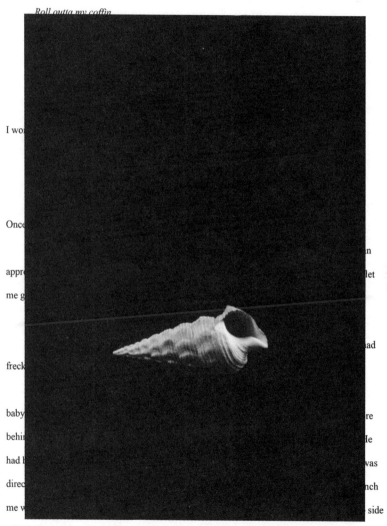

freck   ad

baby   re

behir   le

had l   vas

direc   nch

me v   side

with it. That's when this boy looked over the fence, and I stopped, because it had already been

made extremely clear to me that all of Scott's games were to remain secrets *or else*. But he just looke   ly
dirt b

                                                                                    se
girls
sever

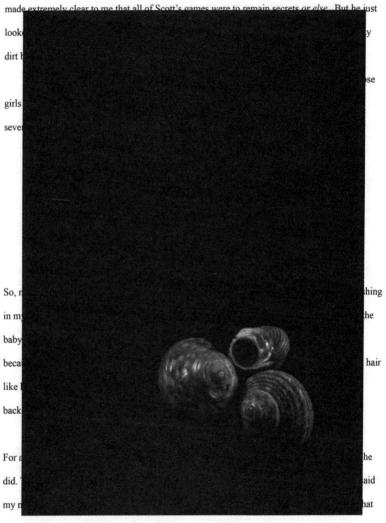

So, n   hing
in my   he
baby
becau   hair
like
back

For a   he
did.   aid
my   hat
he could do to me. I was afraid he would start saying what those things were.

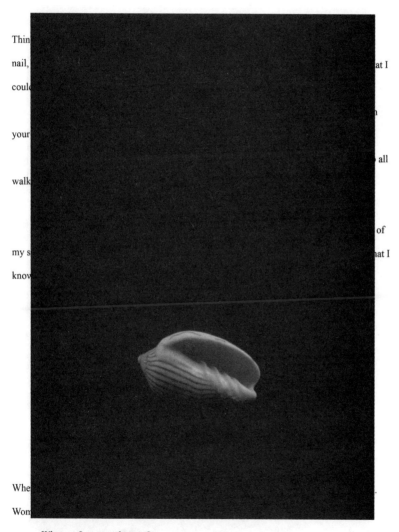

Thin
nail,   at I
coul

your

all
walk

of
my s   at I
know

Whe   .
Wom

What am I supposed to say?

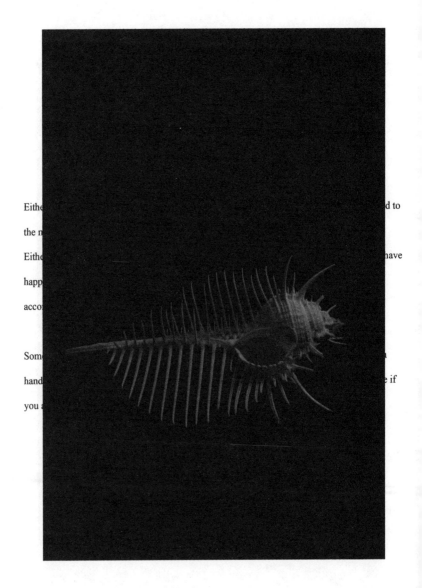

Eith   d to

the n

Eith   have

happ

acco

Som

hand   e if

you a

Words First Seen in Print in 1987, According to Merriam-Webster

Krys Malcolm Belc

1. Potty-mouthed

: *given to the use of vulgar language*

When we met you warned me you liked to curse. Maybe it was more brag than warning. It reminded me of my mother; with her, I was always waiting and cringing. You were brash. I liked it and hated it. It made me remember. My mother cursing at the sink; my mother cursing as she folded our laundry. My mother waiting for me to say, *Mom!* on the other end of the phone after she said something vulgar. When we met, you wanted to get your doctorate in psychology. You wanted to get your doctorate in theater. You wanted to be a psychiatrist. You wanted to move to London and write plays. *And smoke cigarettes*, you said. That part was very important. You were so tall and wanted so many things, but I only wanted you. My mother, too, wanted big things; she was a hardscrabble tennis champion who grew up in Flatbush. *We were the Bad News Bears*, she said, of her team playing the suburban kids. I had never seen the film but I knew what she meant somehow. She got into

Cornell and could not go. It was the money. *I grew up with nothing*, she said. *I was embarrassed to bring my friends over to our apartment. You don't know how lucky you are.* My mother cleaned and cleaned; I can hardly remember her doing anything else. Nothing ever shined enough. The six of us were not allowed to curse. I disappointed my parents greatly, my whole life, but I never cursed in front of them. You did not get your doctorate. You did not write any more plays. You became a nurse. My mother was thrilled. *Nursing, wow, I should have done that*, she said mournfully, folding laundry and looking out the window.

2. BFF

Informal

 : *a very close friend.*

A BFF doesn't gossip about or lie to you. She doesn't share your secrets on her MySpace page.—Girls' Life

Our college rugby team met to make T-shirts. It was silly: the beer, the paints, all of us coloring with fabric pens and signing each other's creations. You left yours behind when you went to work, draped over an auditorium chair. *Oh, crap, Anna's shirt*, a friend said, holding it up to me. *I think she said she was on her way to work*, I said. As if I didn't know for sure. As if I didn't know your hours. We were becoming fast friends, I thought. No one knew; we didn't run in the same crowds. Your emails a secret I didn't know how to explain, our carefully faux-accidental run-ins electric. At the circulation desk I felt everyone's eyes on me as I placed my elbow on the counter, leaned over the scanner to hand you the painted shirt. Where we went to school the library was always crowded, even on a Friday night. People watched me visit you at work. You've always loved to work the latest shift, making money while others relax. Running out the door in your scrubs while I give the kids their after-dinner baths. Saying goodbye as I say goodnight. Dinner: leftovers, Tupperware at 3 a.m. *I'm so glad you brought this back,* you said, stuffing the T-shirt into an enormous purse: you always carry your books in crammed over-the-shoulder bags, never in a backpack.

Girls' school, women's sports: my whole life I'd been falling for my best friends. Legs running downfield, hands that reached into backpacks when I needed to borrow a pen. The way I felt so many friendships obscured by hiding and quietly wanting. The shame and denial. Everyone must feel this way sometimes, I told myself. A group of girls getting ready to go out, a group of girls lacing up to play basketball, big hard shoes over delicate feet, the perfume, the makeup, swigs of alcohol stolen from someone's parents. The high-pitched laughter and hugs I tried to avoid. If they ever find out, I don't want them to think back on this moment, I always thought. I'll sleep on the floor. I'll be the designated driver. Always an intruder. The first time we slept together I used your toothbrush in your dorm bathroom. You laughed. *I guess this is one benefit to sleeping with another woman,* you said, splashing water on your face at the sink next to mine. I laughed too. I always have. When people ask how we met you are sure to tell them we were never friends. This was always a pursuit for you. It's not that it was easy; it is never easy. But you learned this about yourself in college. Pursuit was a freedom.

43

You were never hiding. Nearly eleven years after I brushed my teeth in your dorm bathroom we pull off the Hutchinson Parkway and enter an impossibly small rest stop. The line for the women's room snakes along the wall, and I walk right by it into the men's room. I laugh.

3. Selective Serotonin Reuptake Inhibitor

: *any of a class of antidepressants (such as fluoxetine) that inhibit the inactivation of serotonin by blocking its reuptake by presynaptic neuron endings*

The medication made you not want sex. I was not angry that you were depressed. How could I be angry at that? It was that I needed you even though you said I could go get it anywhere, from anyone. *You're still in college*, you said, *Go find it somewhere else.* You were sad, and you needed the medication, but I was angry. While I studied with my friends or sat alone in my dorm room, headphones on and stacks of books beside me, you stayed in your apartment crying. Your first adult apartment, on Baltimore Avenue. I stained a plain wooden table you bought at IKEA; you had a picture of a couch taped on your living room wall. *It looks like a ballet studio*, you joked. We ate on the floor off paper plates if you had two dinner guests. You had two chairs. You had a handful of mugs and no glasses. I remember all those late night drives to keep you company in your ballet studio. The sex we'd have before I went back to college in the morning, back to class and my dorm. It is embarrassing to admit that I never came with myself before I came with you. You taught me

44

this body was OK. You taught me how to make it work. You grabbed me where I learned to grab myself. It wasn't that I had never tried before, but all I felt was too much flesh in all the wrong places. Fat like what you trim off a roast. Fat for the trash. Fat for the dog's bowl. Fat you peel back, pull taut, slice. *Can I grab you here?* you said. *Can I grab you like this?* you said.

4. Beer Goggles

: the effects of alcohol thought of metaphorically as a pair of goggles that alter a person's perceptions especially by making others appear more attractive than they actually are

You took me out for my first beers when I turned twenty-one. Yards Philly Pale Ale at Standard Tap, at a hipster bar across town from your former ballet studio, which now had a beaten brown couch and walls I had painted Strawberry Rhubarb. We waited on the El tracks looking west at the whole city. *Which way does the train come from again?* I asked, tipsy.

We slept with the woman in your anatomy and physiology class because she and I were drunk and you were curious. At her party everyone trashed her galley kitchen. I remember bottlecaps and crumbled tortilla chips, cigarette butts and the smell of spilled wine and bodies.

Her bed was public. Curtains separated the living room from her massive bedroom, or maybe it was just a flimsy sliding door. I remember a bed with no nightside tables and too many pillows. I remember her

45

name and that she had a big, fluffy cat. Everyone at the party was queer or at least could have been. So many of us in one place. Getting up, cotton-mouthed, to pee. I threw up and went back to sleep next to you, tangled together on the other side of the bed. It is the only time in my life I ever woke up still drunk.

5. Degenderize

: *to eliminate any specific reference to gender in (something, such as a word, text, or act)*

When I am no longer your girlfriend I don't just become your boyfriend. I am in between and I intend to stay that way. I am a partner but come on, people just think that means lesbians, right? I am a lover but people our age do not say that in any kind of seriousness. I have never been a wife or a husband. When my mother has trouble remembering to use the right pronoun you advise: *Just say his name a lot. That's what I do.*

6. In-Line Skate

: *a roller skate whose wheels are set in-line for greater speed and maneuverability*

One of our last dates before you got pregnant was to that roller rink in Camden. You rented a pair of tan roller skates with orange wheels and I paid the extra dollar for black rollerblades. You were no good; I'm not sure why I thought you would be. You looked like a Japanese spider crab on wheels. All limbs and giggles. Smooth hardwood, pop music, lights flashing, crowds of kids. I couldn't help but smile. We had soggy cheese fries and Cokes and watched them with their parents, so impossibly happy, you and me almost like everyone else for at least an hour or two. In-line skates have been around for a long time, maybe centuries. At the National Museum of Roller Skating in Lincoln, Nebraska, you could see skates dating back to 1819. At your high school in New York City, they were supposed to offer Rollerblading Gym your junior year but then September 11th happened and they canceled it. They moved your whole school of over 3,000 kids to another borough, to another school with nearly 5,000 kids. You showed me where you would have bladed, along the Hudson River. When you came back, the Chambers Street subway stop was still full of concrete dust and you signed up for Swim Gym, came early each morning to hit the pool and showed up to your next class with wet, chlorinated hair. It was amazing to me, a school like that just an hour from my high school, which was a big semicircular building in the woods of Bergen County, New Jersey. A giant Jesus was perched outside, watching us come and go. Sometimes when I closed my eyes to go to sleep, hours away at the liberal arts college where I reinvented myself as your lover, I would remember walking down those halls, my kilt and knee socks, feeling so out of place. Soon after I met you, when we were in bed and we heard the metallic whoosh of a low-flying plane on its way to Philadelphia International Airport, which was ten miles from my dorm room, you lost it. I was shocked; you sobbed and shook, your heartbeat that would not slow down, so sudden like that, something I could not understand. Two people, learning to be, in one bed.

I got my first pair of rollerblades after we moved to the suburbs, around the same time I got my first Sony Walkman. Rollerblades were made to get us somewhere, but at eleven and twelve and thirteen I skated the same hundred yards back and forth at the end of Clover Lane. Our house on the edge of eleven acres of marshland, our vast front lawn a wooded bog. Years later, at age thirty, living in small-town Michigan and home to visit I tell my mother how I cannot stand Manhattan, how it always feels like the worst kind of crowded airport, how everyone is always ready to yell at me if I hesitate for just a moment getting onto or off the subway, and she snorts. *You grew up at the end of a cul-de-sac,* she says.

A cul-de-sac they brought me to, when we left Rockaway Beach. We left New York City the year your family arrived from Poland. I was eight, you eleven. You call it your silent year. Everyone at school made fun of my city accent, my off-brand sneakers. They said I looked like the Great Gilly Hopkins, a callous girl from a book we read in class, a girl who hates everyone and everything. Looking back at the book cover Gilly was a classic butch in training, with overalls and a mean face for protection. All the cool kids had their birthday parties where the parents made their kids invite The Whole Class or Else Nobody. I always had a second slice of cake even though eating around all those people pretending to be my friends made me sick. It was something to pass the time. I got AIM a year or two after it launched in 1997. People could sense my desperation even as we all learned to talk to somebody on the internet. My parents had a famously long driveway, maybe the longest in town, and I'd skate back and forth on the smooth pavement listening to music for hours: Green Day, Sarah McLachlan, anything without much happiness to it. It was the only time I was ever really by myself. I didn't know why I needed help calming down but I did. Glide, glide, past days and weeks, tears streaming down my face. I could not really be myself even by myself. Maybe especially by myself.

7. Messenger Bag

: *a rectangular bag that is large enough to carry papers, books, etc., and that usually has a wide shoulder strap and a flap that typically covers the opening and much or all of the front of the bag*

My mother sends me a backpack for school every year, even the years I am a teacher and not a student. You say that you do not like to think of me as a child. *It is too sad*, you say. But I was not always sad; children are resilient. It was not all bad, and so I try to look back for the times my mother said *yes*. No to the Air Jordans for school. No to slacks and a shirt for church. No to haircuts, no to repainting my room red or blue, no to a denim comforter like the ones my brothers had. It made their blankets so heavy, rooted them to their beds. But she said yes to the messenger bag I wanted, instead of a backpack, for the sixth grade. It was silver. In the checkout line she kept asking if I was sure. *It's going to hurt your shoulders, you know*, she said. *It won't*, I said. Maybe we were never quite mother and daughter but in some ways we might have

49

been. I don't remember much from the year of the messenger bag. I got my first Parental Advisory CD, Mase's *Harlem World*, and hid it in my underwear drawer. I forged my mother's signature on a failed science test and it wasn't even close, but I handed it back in to Mr. Gardner anyway and got caught. She had to talk to my French teacher once a week on the phone, to make sure I was doing my homework. One day she came to the school to find all the sweatshirts I had lost and emptied my locker in front of the entire class onto the floor. *Will you believe this?* She asked everyone, looking around as she sifted through an unimaginable pile of junk, bewildered that we could even be related. But it was true: I came right out of her body, on June 27, 1987. We were both there. She was right. The bag hurt my shoulder. I could only really fit one textbook in it, which made it way less likely I'd get it together as a student. The problem didn't last, though; it was so poorly constructed, the fibers connecting the strap to the bag slackened slowly, then snapped, leaving it unfurled on the bottom of my locker one day.

8. FAQ

: *a document (as on a website) that provides answers to a list of typical questions that users might ask regarding a particular subject ("check the FAQ")*

Your father wants to know how I chose the middle name Malcolm. Did I name myself after Malcolm X? It is an accusation. Your father wants to know when you *knew*. Your father wants to know if our kids understand, and if so, how? How do they understand? Why did I bring them to a march? Why did I bring them to a rally? Why can't we just pretend to be normal? Are you sure you've known for this long? It is another accusation. Doesn't this mean no one has to know you're different now? I mean, look at me. Look at me. I almost look normal. Just young. A little soft. Just say this is the way it's always been, that you married a short, impossibly young-looking man. Your father doesn't hug me ever again after I ask you to tell them to call me *he*. *If you liked men so much why didn't you just?*

Someone at your job sees a picture of the five of us, pauses, and asks: *How did you get your kids?* I am surprised when you tell me this at breakfast, over pancakes, after your night shift. No one asks anymore; we are just a mom and a dad and some kids. No one sees anything unusual. Some kids look like their moms; some look like their dads. Sean and ZZ look just like you, Samson looks just like me, and when the three of them sit in a row they look like brothers. Joined by their other genetic half, a man with his own family who lives across the country. *Did Krys have to go off testosterone for that?*

Call your mother, Samson demands one day while I lie on the floor playing Sean's Game Boy. I play Mario and remember the good things about being a little boy. The pings of coins collected, the surprised sound Mario makes when he jumps from wall to wall, surprised at what his little body can do. *Why?* I ask. *I need you to ask her why she made you so HAIRY*, he says. *Your legs are hairy. Your belly is hairy. Your face is hairy. Why did your mother make you so hairy?* His older brother bangs on the bathroom door with both fists while I'm in the shower.

What are you doing in there? he calls out. Samson joins in. *Yeah, what are you doing?*

9. Thirtysomething

: *having an age of 30 to 39 years old* • ***thirtysomething*** *parents;* **also:** *of or relating to people in their thirties*
Just the usual thirtysomething décor—Persian rug, book-shelves, abstract paintings, glass coffee table . . . and a few exotic trinkets picked up on foreign junkets.—Mary Swick

You ask me if you should tell your new therapist that your husband is transgender. You always say *husband* when you think *partner* will be too awkward. *My problems are just not about you,* you say. Your mother has been dead for three weeks. Sometimes you feel like our kids took away your sense of self. Try to read a book and somebody needs their nose blown. You can only drink so many cups of cold tea. Feels like a lie to leave it out, the stuff about me, but who can resist thinking this is everything? The woman who used to be, who should have been, who never was. You married her knowing she was a figment of everyone else's imagination. You said forever when you meant never. Breasts smashed beneath denim shirts, a reluctant Dad who still goes by *Krys*. At home he is just himself with no hoodies, no binders, nothing at all, just boxers and socks. Letters that come from our son's school with his old name on them sit on the counter. Friends who haven't seen us in years forget I won't look anything like they remember. There is no way this could be anything but the most important thing in your life—right? We moved cross country for me to go to graduate school and we do panicked math in the checkout aisles, trying to buy groceries. We can only buy the tiny jars of peanut butter even though each spoonful is more expensive that way. I pick the onions that look like they have lighter skins. The men who live in our house in Philadelphia are getting a divorce and we will need to find new tenants. As far as we can tell one is cheating on the other. We liked them; they decorated and always paid us on time. They fixed our yard door. It is a luxury for millennials to own anything at all, even a house so far away; we know that and desperately want to keep it, our little corner of the world. Your mother never understood or accepted you and now she is dead. You want to know whether you should say something about me to your new therapist in this town a thousand miles from home.

10. Emoticon

: *a group of keyboard characters (such as :-)) that typically represents a facial expression or suggests an attitude or emotion and that is used especially in computerized communications (such as e-mail)*

Is there, like, an MFA in emoticons? you asked after I sent you the following text message: a face with hearts for eyes, an eggplant, a peach, praying hands.

11. Deathcare

: of, relating to, or providing products or services for the burial or cremation of the dead

I did not see your mother when she died. I only saw her in her living coffin, a bed in the middle of the living room where she slept away most of the day. As far as we could tell she was not in pain; her brain went out slowly, like Christmas lights on a string, dimming one by one. We'd never had much to talk about and this day was no different, somehow. I sat in your parents' living room in Queens building an airport out of Duplo blocks, cleaning up as our kids moved from one of your childhood toys to the next. Your parents have never had cable, but the boys found a jar of a hundred tiny Pokemon and dumped it everywhere. Eevee, Magikarp, Mewtwo, Charizard rolling like dice and banging against the foot of the hospital bed. One of my mother's biggest lessons: when you don't know what to do, clean. You kept feeding the kids fruit: quartered grapes, tangerine segments. Each kid took a turn snuggling your mom in her bed. I knew it was my final goodbye when I shuffled our kids out the apartment door, into the hallway where we put our shoes back on. I only waved and said goodbye like always; your mother thanked me for coming, like always. I've always felt that your parents feared I might take you away and never bring you back home. They will never accept that already happened a decade ago. I could not be at the funeral but my mother could; she texted me because she could not remember your mother's name. I called her back to tell her. I had never said it aloud: *Ewa: brings life.*

Becoming

Thirii Myo Kyaw Myint

O f the thirty-one planes of existence, the four realms of imma-
terial forms, the sixteen realms of fine-material forms, and
the eleven realms of sensual forms, humans dwell in the seventh sensual realm, just above hells, animals, hungry ghosts,
and demons.

I was conceived in the short month of hope between the 8888
Uprising on August, 8, 1988, and the bloody coup that followed on
September 18. The Uprising was a general strike organized by university students from Yangon, then called Rangoon, though workers, eth-
nic minorities, Buddhist, Muslim, and Christian leaders soon joined
the ranks. The demonstrations spread all over the country, spread even
to Sittwe, the capital of remote Rakhine State, where my parents were
teaching English. For a brief month, the students at Sittwe Degree College, my parents' students, were marching in the streets too. Then the
military staged a second coup. They declared a state of emergency. They
opened fire on the peaceful protests. General Ne Win said, when the
army shoots, it shoots to hit. Thousands died and thousands more were

injured, were arrested, were tortured, were disappeared. I do not know how many.

My mother and father and elder sisters lived in Sittwe for three years, from 1987 to 1990. They were transferred there from Rangoon as part of a well-intentioned, though ultimately failed, government initiative to send the best governmental employees to the most remote and under-developed regions of the country. My parents were not the first university instructors to be transferred, but they were among the first to accept their assignment, to actually go. We felt a duty to our country, my father says. Duty. Patriotism. Service. Words that create nations. Words that create wars. My parents believed in those words. They believed the Rakhine people were their countrymen and women. They believed in the post-independence dream of a peaceful, multiethnic Burma. A dream that has never come to fruition.

When I was a child, before I knew where or what exactly Sittwe was, I knew that it was a place of exile. As long as I could remember, my family had lived in places where we did not belong, where people asked us where we came from, knowing by the way we looked, or the way we spoke, or perhaps even by some other, more subtle marker that we had come from elsewhere—but my mother and father never spoke of the places where we lived, where I grew up, as places of exile. Sittwe alone was exilic. It was like being sent to prison, my mother always said, like falling into an abyss. The word she used, meaning gorge, pit, or chasm, rhymed with the word meaning fear. Like falling into fear, I heard. On the eve of my conception, my mother said she dreamed of an abyss, a fear into which she had fallen, and a child who lifted her out.

The lowest level of hell is a cube buried deep in the earth. Buried deeper in the earth than the earth's diameter. Buried in an earth only visible to the divine eye. Inside this cube, bodies are packed so tightly together they have no space to move, or even to breathe. They have no space to live, and yet they do. The bodies are alive. This is their punishment.

In the second trimester of my mother's pregnancy, she began to bleed. A threatened abortion. The doctors prescribed bed rest. Universities and colleges all over the country were shut down, so my mother did not even have to take maternity leave from work. She flew back to Rangoon with my two elder sisters. She returned to her parents' house. In the months following the Uprising, the months my mother spent lying in bed, pregnant with me, the military junta whitewashed all the temples in Rangoon. To cleanse the country, they said. To prepare for a new beginning. It was to cover the evidence of their slaughter. The bloodstains on the temple walls and floors.

Before she left for Rangoon, my mother consulted a holy man and he foretold that Sittwe would be the place of my death. If I was ever brought back to the city, he said, the land would swallow me. I would be buried in the ground, and all my family after me. The ground that was glutted with the bodies of so many Rakhine and so many Bamar. The ground upon which blood had so recently been spilled. The ground that would swallow more bodies in years to come.

I do not know how my mother found this holy man. I do not know how I could ever find him again. Perhaps she only met him in another dream. She called him bodaw, a title of respect, and it is the only name by which I know him, this man who saved my life. He was not a mortal man, but a healer, as old as the forests in which he lived. His was a wisdom older than the pre-colonial kingdoms, the divisions of people, older even than any religion.

The lives of animals are visible to the human eye. A fat hog tied up by the road, the mud drying black on her back. Lying so still she might be dead. Or, the oxen working in the fields. Or, the street dogs come to scavenge a roadkill. Or, the roadkill itself, its entrails scattered in the dirt. To celestial beings, human lives seem as short as the lives of animals seem to us. In one story, the awakened one overturns a stone and points to the maggots crawling underneath. These will be humans thousands of years from now, the awakened one says.

I was born on the sixth day of the waxing moon in Nayon, the third month of the Burmese year. It was the beginning of the rainy season. By the Gregorian calendar, I was born in June 1989, the month the military junta, which had recently renamed itself SLORC, the State Law and Order Restoration Council, changed all the names in the country as well. Rangoon became Yangon, and Burma became Union of Myanmar. A few days after my birth, I developed neonatal jaundice and the doctors recommended that I be kept at the hospital for treatment. My mother refused. My father, who had returned to Rangoon, now called Yangon, built a makeshift light therapy station for me at my grandparents' house. A month later, the Rains Retreat, Vassa, began. Two days after that, the leaders of the opposition party, the National League for Democracy, and hundreds of other political detainees were sentenced, by a military tribunal, to long prison terms or to death.

The first time I returned to Yangon, my little cousin swung a metal pipe in the front yard of my grandparents' house, and it hit my eldest sister, and she bled, and cried, and believed she would be poisoned by the rust. That night, and every night after that, during our visit, she had terrible, fevered dreams, dreams that infected me and my middle sister since we slept beside her beneath the same mosquito net. Collectively, we dreamed of the crawl space underneath the house, the darkness there, red screams, and the glint of metal. My mother said the house was cursed. The house where she grew up, on a tree-lined street with a wrought-iron gate and jasmines blooming in the garden. The house where she lived with her father and mother even after she was married, even after she had given birth to her first child. The house where that child had fallen ill. The house he never returned to.

The second time I returned, it was the eve of the twentieth anniversary of the 8888 Uprising. My mother always said I might have been reincarnated from one of the student protestors, because I was born ten months after the Uprising and nine months after the bloody coup that followed. My mother did not like to imagine that I had suffered a violent death, but I romanticized the Uprising and the young people who had died for it—shot down in the streets, suffocated in a police van, or executed in the prison yard. I liked to imagine this was the brief life I had before this one, the life of an activist, a revolutionary, a martyr.

Demons live in the celestial realms during the day and in the hell realms during the night. In this way, they can also be called fallen or dark angels. They are visible to angels and angels are visible to them. Sometimes planes of existence coexist. Like celestial beings, demons experience immense pleasure, and like the inhabitants of hell, they experience immense pain. Unlike humans, they cannot experience indifference or equanimity. Their passions are always exaggerated and become their faults: pride, envy, jealousy, wrath.

The monk asked me, did I want him to read my fortune? and I knew it was a trick question because monks did not tell fortunes. Holy men believed in karma, not superstition. My mother always said so before she gave a reading of any kind, and my father always said so when he wanted to wash his hair on a Wednesday. I did not know how to answer the monk. I could feel my whole family watching me, waiting for me to speak. Finally, the monk said, here is your fortune. You will grow old. You will get sick and you will die. I knew, even then, that the monk was wrong. Many people do not grow old or get sick. They just die.

A few years ago, I made a list of everyone I knew who had died, in chronological order. My uncle who died of liver failure. My grandmother who died of diabetes. My grandfather who died of old age. My friend in high school who died in a car accident when the driver fell asleep at the wheel. Another uncle who also died of liver failure. A boy in my freshman year dorm who fell off the roof of a building and died. A girl in my anthropology class who was reported dead, though I never found out how she died. My aunt who had a heart attack. A friend of a friend who walked into the bay and drowned himself. A boy I knew from college who once told me he sometimes looks around a crowded room and wonders, who will love me? He was found dead on the subway tracks at four in the morning.

And before all these deaths, my brother died. His death the first death in my life, though it occurred before my life began.

Sometimes, late at night, the wind sounds like a hungry ghost. Like all of its sorrow is pushed through a pinprick mouth. A mouth that will fit only a single grain of rice. A mouth that will never take in enough food to fill its cavernous stomach. Hungry ghosts wander the same plane as humans and animals, and dogs will bark at them, but most of us cannot see the ghosts. For this, they are grateful. The hungry ghosts are creatures of shame. They are ashamed by their hunger, and by their inability to satiate their hunger. Some of them are hungry for that which is shameful: excrement, rotting flesh, vomit.

The first time my eldest sister pushed a finger down her throat, she said she thought of our brother, and how he had died because he vomited up all of his milk, because he could not drink, take nourishment, and grow. All the days he was in the hospital, my mother prayed that he would live. She was not allowed to see him at the hospital. My father and my grandparents would not allow it. They believed that women who had recently given birth were in a delicate state, a precarious state, of soft blood and soft skin, and in this state, they were close to madness. My father and my grandparents believed my mother had to be shielded from any shock or disturbance. And my brother's body had been shocking, my mother said, when she finally saw him at the children's hospital, in an incubator at the NICU. She hardly recognized him. He had been a fair, chubby baby, a handsome boy, and now he looked like a shriveled animal, so many tubes and wires sticking out of his little body. He would have fit in the palm of her hand, my mother said, her small, slender hand. But she was not allowed to hold him.

I never found the jars of vomit hidden in the closet I shared with my two sisters, but I always knew the closet was haunted. I always made sure the closet door was closed before I went to bed. My eldest sister vomited in jars because there was only one bathroom between the five of us and it was not easy for her to hide her illness. Sometimes, though, she did not bother to hide it at all, and sometimes she used it as a weapon against my mother. She would lock herself in the bathroom in the middle of a fight, and neglect to turn on the fan, so that my mother could hear what my sister was doing in there, so she would be sorry for whatever she had said. I remember watching my sister on her knees in the kitchen one evening. The cabinet door below the sink swinging open, the trash pulled out, and my sister's head bent over it. My mother said ghosts eat out of dumpsters and I believed my sister was possessed. I do not know what excuse my sister gave me but I remember I did not believe it. I was old enough to recognize a lie. I said, I've puked only once in my life. Keep watching me, my sister said, and you'll be able to vomit too.

The first time my eldest sister pushed a finger down her throat she thought of my brother and how he had died, how she had died, because that was the worst thing that had happened to her, that had happened to all of us daughters, long before we were born, and when she made herself vomit, it was as if she were bringing him back to life, by reliving his death, as if she were aborting him over and over again, so that in the moment before she bent her head over the toilet, or the trash in the kitchen, or the glass jar in her hands, in the dark of the closet, he was alive again, at the back of her throat, a ghost waiting to be born.

There are poignant metaphors for the rareness of a human birth. A needle thrown from the earth and a needle thrown from the sky. A blind turtle surfacing once a century and a yoke floating over the five oceans of the world. The needles meet midair and the turtle lifts its head through the yoke. This is how we are all conceived.

The night I turned ten, I felt sad. I remember kneeling on the bed I shared with my sisters after we had said our prayers as we did every night, and thinking to myself: I won't make it to a hundred. Long life was one of the things my mother taught me to pray for. Good health, happiness, safety, the fulfillment of all our family's needs and wants. I was taught to pray for my parents to win the lottery, for us to be able to live in a big house and own a nice car. The night I turned ten, I had something like a premonition as I said my prayers. My parents will never win the lottery. We will never move out of apartments. We will never own a decent car. I felt tired of wanting things. Life seemed very long. I did not want to live to a hundred.

That night at the hospital, my mother changed her prayers. She no longer prayed for my brother's life, she said, but for an end to his suffering.

To this day, I have vomited only once in my life. I remember little of the incident, only having gone to bed nauseous, then waking up in the middle of the night, and suddenly my parents were there in the bathroom with me, my father holding me up by the sink, and the feeling of disgust and relief when I dribbled out a yellowish paste. It felt like crying, but even better and even worse, and still half-asleep it was all a dream or a nightmare: my father's hands gripping my armpits, the fluorescent light above the mirror, and the shadows everywhere else.

Dreaming of Ramadi in Detroit

Aisha Sabatini Sloan

When we get to the Dallas airport, the televisions are showing a headline about a hunter who paid hundreds of thousands of dollars to kill an endangered rhinoceros. It makes me feel a screech inside, a smearing. "Don't look," Hannah warns me, but I keep erupting in puffs of indignity on the escalator. At the gate, I cry at the end of the Das Racist song "Rainbow in the Dark," when Victor Vazquez says, "We tried to go to Amsterdam they threw us in Guantanamo." Then I play it over again so I can trip back into my cry.

As if on cue, CNN reports that a bunch of Bin Laden's documents have been discovered. He reminds me, in one clip, of a boy I went to college with, whose eyes were huge and kind and beautiful like a superpower. There is room for empathy in the reporting, which I find a little terrifying. These news anchors have been given this kind of permission, or the order, to humanize what once was our monster. The "why" behind these gusts of change in media seems just as disconcerting to me, sometimes, as the news itself.

The anchors highlight Bin Laden's concern that his followers should not try to create a caliphate. That he loved his children. The word "achingly" is used. They speak of love letters to his wives. His fear of drones. It reminds me of that weird swoon of time when I couldn't stop watching *Homeland* because of the feeling of vertigo I got when the kind-eyed terrorist lost his son to a drone. Tonight, I will dream that I live in a city like the recently captured Ramadi. We have to make deals with the soldiers, who hold items on a pillow as we haggle for our lives.

The last time I flew into Detroit, I saw a famous man whom I thought was Delroy Lindo. Airport employees came up to him, held his shoulder, joked with him. On screens, CNN was reporting the non-indictment ruling in Missouri and I felt a special honor to watch with this famous black man those first reports from Ferguson, when Ferguson *became* Ferguson, as Michael Brown's stepfather shouted, "Burn this bitch down!" into a crowd.

On the plane, I sat across the aisle from, as Percival Everett might call him, Not Delroy Lindo, who was, nonetheless, *somebody*, as an engineer was called onto the plane to fix a piece of ceiling that was popping off in the corner. After what felt like an unnecessary eternity of duct taping, we began to move, and when the plane picked up speed the ceiling actually fell down. The ceiling of a portion of the plane fell down onto people's shoulders, and we screamed "STOP STOP!" But the pilot sitting next to me, because a lot of airline staff happened to be riding that day, laughed and said, "It's much more dangerous to stop than whatever threat that ceiling poses. That's cosmetic." So we lifted into the air and people, unbuckled, stood up to hold the ceiling together, and Not Delroy Lindo chuckled with the girl to his left, and I felt more comfortable with the calamity because he was there. Not Delroy Lindo's scarf fell and I handed it to him, managing not to say, "Mr. Lindo." It was so soft.

On this trip home, I have been texting with my cousin, who tells me that I will not be able to shadow her at work while I'm visiting. It would have been my second time on a ride-along with her on her rounds as a lieutenant for Detroit's 9th precinct. So much has changed since the first time. Namely, I have developed an instinctive sense of terror upon seeing police cars, triggered by the footage of black men being killed by white officers that lurk in every seam of screen, videos stirred to life the same way that advertisements in the margins come alive when you scroll down or accidentally hover your mouse. But instead of saying "FIND A DENTIST IN TUCSON," it's a death showing. A death is showing. Like a pregnancy or a film or some underwear.

Rather than being shot at, my new fear would be of seeing the officers unleash violence upon a helpless body, having to watch within the confines of my approximated uniform, padded with a bulletproof vest, which would incontrovertibly claim me, identify my orientation toward the police and not the helpless body, drown me out even though I can't imagine that I wouldn't be screaming, I am the kind of person who screams. And aren't I? Affiliated? My cousin is my cousin. She's my blood. But so am I black. My father is black. She's white. But her children are black. Our affiliations are bleeding all over the place.

The last time I was home, which was the first time that Detroit functioned as my home-home since my parents moved from Los Angeles last year, my father and I rode to Target together for some groceries. I was writing about Spaulding Gray on my laptop as we crossed a stretch of road that only my father would think to take at this time of night, his instincts for navigating his hometown so seamless, and we coasted across the black bridge, the black night, through the black city. On the way back, we noticed the farmer's market blockade separating Grosse Pointe from Detroit along Alter Road, and we were pontificating about segregation as we approached an intersection. The light went green and we started to move and I heard gunshots and saw a house full of people leak into the street—the girl in pink sweatpants hiding behind an SUV—and I said, "DAD, GO. THERE WERE GUNSHOTS. KEEP DRIVING. DRIVE FASTER." But he heard SOMETHING ELSE and so, for the love of god, we stopped in front of the SUV that was hiding a young woman from a bullet. GO GO GO! I shouted and my father said, "I thought you said to stop," and as we drove farther and farther away we were reenacting the conversation and laughing harder each time. "I was like, GO FASTER." "And I was all, you want me to stop?" Meanwhile, the scene kept spilling out in time.

At the house, the radio is playing in my attic bedroom to scare away the squirrels that enter by way of a hole in the bathroom. A piece of insulation is reaching through a hole in the ceiling from a rain leak and it looks like a squirrel's reaching arm. Rihanna welcomes me to my bedroom by saying, "Bitch better have my money," and I prepare to take a shower.

The night before Thanksgiving, I went downstairs and my cousin the lieutenant was cooking even though she had to wake up at 6 a.m. to go to work, where she would be encountering Ferguson-inspired protesters "who don't even live here." Upstairs, I paced and paced because I was supposed to write something for the Black Life Matters conference when I got back to Arizona. Facebook was ablaze with anger. Every status update sounded to me like a call for my cousin to die. I thought about surveillance and wondered if we were being lured into action by an unseen man in a suit somewhere. I was convinced that everyone's anger would end up benefiting the GOP. I began to write a series of posts that I never posted, "Let's boycott social media!" "Let's read Noam Chomsky!" and "What if this is the Pentagon's experiment to track the time it takes for a Facebook post to turn into a violent act!" I scream in the face of most things, I guess. But then I watched the video of Eric Garner being strangled and I cried and I couldn't stop for hours.

On one episode of *The Ali G Show*, Sacha Baron Cohen asks Andy Rooney a bunch of stupid questions, one of which is does the newspaper ever report something that hasn't happened yet like an election or a plane crash. Andy Rooney is apoplectic, he is DONE, and he spits, "How do you know what the news is? If it hasn't happened yet?" which I've always taken to be a kind of fatal oversight, the moment when the satirical clouds shift and truth is revealed, like when the rap ends and the song is no longer a sexy joke and the rapper who went to Wesleyan is imagining over top no beat that he could be thrown into Guantanamo when he was just trying to be a stoned hipster.

For my family, Detroit has always been inevitable. It is the place we have been heading back to my entire life. My parents recall White Castle hamburgers and Coney Island hot dogs as if they were the secret to immortality. The city has the beckoning power of a black hole or the

Italian countryside or a castle. There is no way to explain our wiring to someone whose fairy tale has always ended somewhere like Florida. Recently, a new friend kept scrunching up her nose when I said my family moved from California to Detroit. This happens all the time. But in this moment it hit me that one of the things that makes no sense when people ask "WHY DETROIT?" with all of their death showing is this presumption that we can choose our homes.

Architectural Survey Form: 902 Sunset Strip

Camellia–Berry Grass

MISSOURI DEPARTMENT OF NATURAL RESOURCES
STATE HISTORIC PRESERVATION OFFICE, P.O. Box 176, Jefferson City, MO 65102
ARCHITECTURAL/HISTORIC INVENTORY FORM

1. Survey No. CL-AS-7–18		2. Survey name: Excelsior Springs Historic Resources	
3. County: Clay		4. Address (Street No.) 902	Street (name) Sunset Strip
5. City: Excelsior Springs	Vicinity: ☐	6. Geographical Reference: 39.358275, -94.229861	7. Township/Range/Section: T: 52N R: 30W S:1
8. Historic name (if known): Grass Residence; Garden House; Connie's House; The One With The Birdfeeders; Twice-Yearly Garage Sale; Flamingo Flock; Connie's Bar & Grill		9. Present/other name (if known): It's not Connie's anymore.	
10. Ownership: ☒ Private ☐ Public	11a. Historic use (if known): Horror and refuge. It was wet with booze breath & then verdant with root-growth. Less desperate than it was. Decorated.	11b. Current use? Unknown. After mom passed the property changed owners, an unfamiliar red truck visible in the driveway on Google Maps, renovated with white shiplap, all the music taken out of it.	

HISTORICAL INFORMATION

12. Construction date: 1971	15. Architect: n/a	18. Previously surveyed? ☐ Cite survey name in box 22 cont. (page 3)
13. Significant date/period: 1992–2016	16. Builder/contractor: n/a	19. On National Register? ☐ individual ☐ district Cite nomination name in box 22 cont. (page 3)
14. Area(s) of significance: AGRICULTURE; HEALTH/ MEDICINE; LAW	17. Original or significant owner: Connie Grass	20. National Register eligible? ☐ individually eligible ☐ district potential (☐ C ☐ NC) ☐ not eligible not determined
21. History and significance on continuation page. ☐		22. Sources of information on continuation page. ☐

MISSOURI DEPARTMENT OF NATURAL RESOURCES
STATE HISTORIC PRESERVATION OFFICE, P.O. Box 176, Jefferson City, MO 65102
ARCHITECTURAL/HISTORIC INVENTORY FORM   Page 86

ARCHITECTURAL INFORMATION

23. Category of property: ☐ building(s) ☐ site ☐ structure ☐ object	30: Roof material: Asphalt shingle	37.Windows: ☐ historic ☐ replacement Pane arrangement:
24. Vernacular or property type:	31. Chimney placement: Offset left	38. Acreage (rural): Visible from public road? ☐
25. Architectural Style: Split-level Ranch style	32. Structural system: Wood frame	39. Changes (describe in box 41 cont.): ☐ Addition(s) Date(s): ☐ Altered Date(s):
26. Plan shape: Rectangular	33. Exterior wall cladding: Brick and lumber	☐ Moved Date(s): ☐ Other Date(s): Endangered by:
27. No. of stories: 1 Front 2	34. Foundation material: Unknown	Drought. Flood.
28. No. of bays (1st floor): Seven	35. Basement type: Full	40. No. of outbuildings (describe in box 40 cont.):
29. Roof type: Truncated Hip	36. Front porch type/placement: Platform	41. Further description of building features and associated resources on continuation page. ☐

OTHER

42. Current owner/address: [Redacted]	43.Form prepared by (name and org.): [the woman who had a gross boyhood here, with a name that no longer fits]	44. Survey date: 2018 45. Date of revisions:

FOR SHPO USE

Date entered in inventory:	Level of survey ☐ reconnaissance ☐ intensive	Additional research needed? ☐ yes ☐ no
National Register Status: listed in listed district Name: ☐ pending listing ☐ eligible (individually) ☐ eligible (district) ☐ not eligible ☐ not determined	Other:	

MISSOURI DEPARTMENT OF NATURAL RESOURCES
STATE HISTORIC PRESERVATION OFFICE, P.O. Box 176, Jefferson City, MO 65102
ARCHITECTURAL/HISTORIC INVENTORY FORM   Page 87

LOCATION MAP (include north arrow)	**LOCATION PHOTOGRAPH** (taken Oct. 2013)
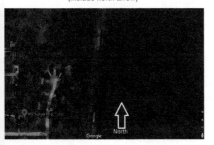	

PHOTOGRAPH

Photographer: Google Street View	Date: Oct. 2013	Description Fall color masks the state of browning, the wilting walls of plants cradling every post, a long makeshift fence of bushes, nothing upright without plants encircling its base.

ADDITIONAL INFORMATION:

21. (cont.) History and significance.
Expand box as necessary, or add continuation pages.

Because to voice the desire to escape would only bring his fist. Desire disturbs the air in the house, thickens the place like roux, and dad would swat and swat as if clearing smoke. In the Midwest we value the Privacy of the Domestic Sphere. "Adults can do whatever they want as long as they keep it in the privacy of their own bedroom," say all of the good men and women in town, over their shoulders to their children, at even the slightest hint of queerness. They lump queerness in with the actual perils they allow the home to cover up: the screaming, the recycling full of aluminum cans, the shattered plates, the craters in the drywall.

The significance of this house is the lesson that nothing private stays. You can only live in town for so long before other people's parents hear about your dad's drinking. You can only go to school for so long before people begin to wonder about the bruises. Life in the rural Midwest is a timeline of when private experiences are made public. Only your internality can escape.

We moved into 902 Sunset Strip from a castle-gray box on N. Kimball because my parents wanted more room for me & my brother. Or maybe just for herself. My mom painted the front room clay-orange & hung southwestern landscapes on the walls. And what she meant to say to me, to everyone in the house, even my dad, every neighbor that visited, what she meant by this was: *I have been depleted by this man and this life but I will raise these children and I will teach my students. I want more than what I have. I am emptied but I am vast.* And when the orange gave way to peapod green, she was speaking to us again: *I will outlive you because unlike you, there is bloom in me yet.*

In the years after the divorce, my mom would begin to plant shrubs and perennials and tomatoes and big blossoms around the entire perimeter of the property, lining every bit of fence with something green. And I know she was making friends on music message boards. And I know from reading her journals after she passed away that she was dating. And I know that her reputation was turning around from "the teacher with the awful husband" and "the woman who runs the best garage sale in town" to "the wild plant lady." But this was speech, unvoiced. Seeds planted and soil nurtured and speech harvested. She was trying to tell us that she was growing.

By the time she told me about her cancer diagnosis, the front room and the bedroom and the kitchen had taken on a beach theme. New England shore kitsch lined the shelves in the kitchen and the other rooms were inspired by Floridian aesthetics. We never talked about how scared she was, or how she felt about dying. But she was telling me something by manifesting shell and seaspray around her. She was saying: *This is where I hope to be soon, one way or another. On the edge of worlds and, with politeness toward the waves, finally, taken in.*

40. (cont.) Description of environment and outbuildings.
Expand box as necessary, or add continuation pages.

Home located in a late 1960s or early 1970s subdivision on the westernmost part of town. This subdivision, not formally named, was built around Peachtree Street, Dogwood Street, Apple Blossom Street, Michele Street, Milwaukee Street, and Miss Belle Street. It was intended to be a more affordable neighborhood compared to the more deluxe planned subdivision in western

MISSOURI DEPARTMENT OF NATURAL RESOURCES
STATE HISTORIC PRESERVATION OFFICE, P.O. Box 176, Jefferson City, MO 65102
ARCHITECTURAL/HISTORIC INVENTORY FORM   Page 89

Excelsior Springs, King's Edition, which was next to the hospital. Home is located near the Canadian Pacific Railway line, which ran through thick forest that could take you all the way to Salem Road, past city limits. The train would shake the walls of the house and the Jewel tea dishes would rattle and it was a reminder that it was possible to move forward, to leave. Home had consistent yellow paint with blue trim.

Home was in the middle of a short block of three homes total; Connie Grass had made a de facto fence for the front-facing side of the property by planting a wide variety of plants along each property line; a deliberate differentiation from the well-kept lawns and lack of front fencing in the rest of the neighborhood. It is unclear whether the plants were there for her protection or for the protection of her neighbors.

41. (cont.) Description of primary resource.
Expand box as necessary, or add continuation pages.

The bedroom of the oldest child was sky blue for a number of years, but was painted black during their adolescence. After moving out, it became a peach-hued museum hosting Connie's collection of concert photos and musicians' autographs. Its final stage was a Thomas the Tank Engine-themed room for Connie's grandson.

The basement, nominally a recreation room, was a mixture of lime green paint and wood paneling. The music museum took its place down here when Connie's youngest child had a son. The museum expanded. The front room and kitchen first took on an American Southwest/*Arizona Highways* feel, with sandy-colored walls and framed images of buttes and mesas. It would, as if a drought reversed, become greener and greener over the years, as plants and framed pictures of Anne Geddes's photography replaced the more arid decorations. Its final stage was an embrace of Florida Keys chic: seashore village romanticism and Margaritaville-style resort town aesthetics. The garage was never used to store vehicles. It hosted garage sales once, sometimes twice a year, for necessary supplemental income. Connie would try to sell any and every toy or shirt that wasn't getting frequent use. If the contents of the home are self-expression, the garage served as a way to store expressive acts that no longer served a use. A warehouse of discarded desire.

The present occupants of the home have painted every room white and gray-mauve. White shiplap blankets the entryway and kitchen. New faux-marble countertops and quaint "country" fixtures adorn the kitchen. Everything looks as if draped by the veil of a ghost.

Egg Face

Hea-Ream Lee

My face is peeling. I bring the back of my hand to meet my cheek and when I rub, white flakes of skin peel up and slough off in little rolls. I used to try to mitigate this with moisturizer, spackling thick creams and pastes onto my dry skin like impasto on canvas. I'd smear on oils, viscous and shiny and aromatic, sucked out of apothecary bottles with little glass droppers. But now I know once the skin starts to peel there is nothing to be done except help it along.

Sometimes I want to take the industrial-strength green Korean loofah, my sandpapery mitten, and just scrub at my face until huge chunks of flesh tear away and roll into brown fleshy noodles and fall to the floor. Afterward, I won't be bloody and flayed, all raw nerve endings and hamburger meat, I'll be smooth as a peeled egg, soft and firm and pliant to the touch.

When I was a girl I went through a ghost story phase. Not white people ghost stories, which I felt immune to somehow—another thing, like being grounded and getting Cs, that didn't apply to me—but Korean ghost stories, starring young female specters in white robes with long, bedraggled black hair. One of them involved a ghost who was often glimpsed from behind on dark mountain paths, her limbs luminescent in the moonlight. When a traveler would catch up to her, wondering why a beautiful young woman was wandering the mountains alone, she would spin around and her face would be totally blank, no features. She's the 달걀귀신, the egg ghost, terrifying because you have no idea how she feels, and isn't that the most dangerous kind of woman?

My mom and I talk on the phone and the last thing she tells me is to wear sunscreen and a hat. *Always*, she says. Lest my face go wrinkly, lest my visage be marred by a spray of sunspots, lest my features sink into the vast plain of my face, eyes like gleaming stones in a dried-up streambed.

Lately I find myself falling silent in professional settings, in class-rooms, casual conversations. A self-inflicted erasure, a scrubbing away of words and thoughts and ideas. I wish I could locate this muteness, prod it the way I once dissected fibrous gray owl pellets in science class as a kid, metal probes gently teasing apart the clot of tissue until I could see tiny mouse bones, delicate and pearly white, amid the fluff. What part of my silence is who I am, and what part is how I was brought up? What part is external, structural, the part that tells me I am other, and therefore undeserving of a voice? What part of it is about a desire for control, a fear of being misunderstood?

Nobly born Korean children in the Goryeo dynasty used to wash their faces with an essence made from peach blossoms. This was said to make their complexions as clear and light as white jade. Koreans' obsession with flawless skin, that is to say, pale skin, that is to say, white skin, predated the country's growing postwar obsession with Western beauty ideals by millennia.

I think about Korean farmers in agrarian times wearing full faces of makeup—thick layers of foundation and eyeshadow—to protect them from the sun as they bent in rice paddies, submerged to the knees.

I ask my Korean friends about this story, believing it to be common if apocryphal, and to my surprise, they don't know it, nor can I locate any trace of it on the internet. I always assumed it was my mom who told it to me when I was a child, but when I ask, she has no idea what I'm talking about. Was it something I read in a book? Was it something I made up, the natural outpocketing of a desire to connect to the people who looked like me, who seemed so far away? The agglomeration of a life lived in skin, the accumulated debris of two societies to which whiteness equals beauty, purity, power? I touch my face and it's like I'm standing in the rice paddy, too. I can almost feel the perfectly winged eyeliner and pale, flawless cheeks turned to the sun, unmarred by the sweat of hard labor. I feel the swish of cool water around my calves, the warm cloth stretched across my back as I work and I'm protected and strong, and beautiful I suppose.

To me, female Korean beauty is really about silence. About demureness, about winnowing oneself down not through exercise, which would yield unsightly musculature, but through self-denial. Or through surgery, the skin of the face peeled up and the bones underneath broken and ground down and fused and then blanketed again with the skin, always the skin. A certain slimness of the limbs, a sexless and pure kind of silence. It's about being unthreatening, about emotional blankness conveyed through blurred eyeshadow, or blush buffed out just so. A beauty of a certain kind of body, a certain kind of whiteness—not Whiteness exactly, but whiteness nonetheless.

But who am I to say? I'm not Korean, not really. Not quite American either, of course. Can you hate something and still, shamefully, desire it?

Someday I'll be beautiful, with panna cotta skin, poreless like a puddle of milk. Someday my face will gleam, luminous, and that light will get brighter and brighter until you can't see my dark eyes, my smudge of a mouth, until all that is visible is the contour of my face, an oval of resplendent light, and I'll turn and all will regard my beauty and my terrible, terrible silence.

Fragments, Never Sent

Molly McCully Brown

Dear F,

Throughout high school and college, when I was trying to be a writer, I also tried, regularly, to be a person who kept notebooks, because I understood it is what writers do: Joan Didion at the *hotel bar, Wilmington RR* on an *August Monday morning*. Our father, always with a black Moleskine and a bleeding Pilot pen. I knew I was supposed to be paying attention, taking notes, feeling my head fill up with fragments of language I couldn't afford to forget. So I bought journals, and began them, and left them off, and bought others, and did it again. It's not surprising I was never any good at it: It's hard for me to write more than a few sentences by hand before my spastic fingers start to hurt, and then my wrist, and then my arm if I press on for long enough. And, anyway, I'm too precious about objects, too opposed to error, for that kind of record keeping: the whole book always seemed ruined once one page was ugly, or false-started, or banal. But that's less than half the story. I still have all those partial notebooks, boxed up in a storage unit with the rest of what I own, because I am a writer now, and working on a project somewhere between permanent addresses. And, though I haven't really looked at them in years, I know that nearly every started page is fashioned not just as a note, or fragment, or idea, but as a letter meant for you. They all begin *Dear Frances, Dear Franny, Dear F, Dear Sister, Dear Ghost.*

Then, mostly, I go on to talk about the weather, or the book I'm reading, something I overheard, someone I'm drawn to: as if you know what *summer* is, or *September,* or *coffee* or the *radio* or *Jupiter* or a *bruise* or the *stretch of Highway 1 that runs up California's coast.* As if you've ever seen a *cliff.* Everything is something I want to tell you. Or, the whole world feels remarkable when I imagine you in it. Or, often when I'm bored, or crabby, I remember you are dead and have never run your fingers through your hair, or lit a match, or looked out of a car window, or heard anybody call for you across a room, and that knowledge makes things sharp and worthwhile again.

But, after a few paragraphs of any letter, I always run into the fact that I don't know you at all. That you're just a figure I've made up in relief against myself. An imaginary friend, continually conjured way past childhood. An absence I've spent a lifetime papering around. You're just the page, and anything I write to you is selfish. You're a way to lend more weight to what I'm saying to the air.

*

Dear F,

I've been collecting stories about separated twins since I was old enough to look for them. Castor and Pollux hatch from a single egg and grow up riding white horses of foam formed by the ocean waves. When Castor dies in battle, Pollux asks to be a star positioned alongside him rather than go on living alone. Given the choice, he'd rather keep his brother than his body. In an updated *Parent Trap*, which I watched hundreds and hundreds of times, two versions of Lindsay Lohan discover one another at summer camp. They reunite their parents, do the rest of their growing up together. In a newspaper article, two brothers, adopted to different families at birth, know nothing about one another. They are both named Jim. They both get married twice, first to women named Linda, then to women named Betty. They pick up identical smoking habits; they both have dogs named Toy. They live forty-five miles apart, but don't meet until they're 39. They discuss their identical tension headaches and woodworking hobbies. Move in next door to one another. Are never apart again.

When I was a child, I used to imagine one day I'd discover you were out there somewhere living a parallel life. I wanted your death to be a fiction because then my loneliness would be a fiction. And, *look*, I've done it again, arrived already at the selfishness of missing who you could have been for me.

*

Dear F,

Sometimes I think I want to make a list of the things you did feel, and know, when you were alive, those hours when you were. Right here in the world. *The air. The fabric of a hospital blanket. The skin on more than*

97

one set of hands. The small heat another body makes while it holds you. But the list is only solid and comforting like that for a moment before it includes: *The heart monitor yowling. A tube down your tiny throat. Pressure. Electrodes peeling off your skin. Pain. The burning when you can't breathe.* I've had so many tubes down my throat, when I was old enough to recall them. I want none of that for you. I wrote, once, that I wanted a body for you, and it's true. But this is what our body means, as much as any of the rest of it. I should say *bodies.* But now there's only mine and the way it holds the ghost of yours.

*

Dear F,

This is my second year of living, essentially, out of a suitcase. Two Julys ago I paid two men and their wives to pack up the apartment where I'd lived through graduate school and move everything I own into an improbably small storage unit off a highway on the outskirts of a town in Mississippi: All my books, my framed artwork; my bed and the bulk of my clothing; the huge, cheap corkboard where, for years, I'd pinned drafts of poems in progress and postcards from people I loved. I left my guitar there; the black cowboy boots I'd bought and had refurbished when I lived in Texas; the two stuffed sheep that belonged to the two of us in the NICU, wrapped in a blanket, safely in their own box. They're the only thing I own that you ever touched.

I spent a few weeks visiting our parents in Virginia, and then ten months in Arkansas for a short-term job at a literary magazine. Before

I arrived, the magazine's staff outfitted an apartment for me, furnished with donations, garage sale finds, and the labor of volunteers. Because they were kind and conscientious, and because they knew the move was jarring and disorienting in the way such temporary relocations often are, they devoted a lot of attention to ensuring the apartment didn't feel sterile and staged. They hung framed paintings on the walls, left a woven throw-blanket on the couch and a blue clay rooster with wire legs on the little kitchen table. The whole place was haphazard and warm, but without any of my own things, it had the effect of making me feel, in the months I lived there, as if I'd stepped into the frame of someone else's life, someone with their own particular taste, and rhythms, and eccentricities. On the phone with friends, I joked wryly that I sometimes had the sensation I'd ousted the apartment's previous inhabitant and just assumed her life in the middle of a workweek; sat down on her beat-up green couch, used her checkered oven mitts, her scuffed blender, her blue poly-blend towels as if they belonged to me, as if no one would notice I had taken her place.

What I didn't tell anyone: Occasionally, I convinced myself the room around me was filled not with the cast-offs of strangers, but with things you had accumulated and loved. That it was your life I'd stepped suddenly into the center of: quotidian, tangible, ongoing. I picked up the soap dish in the bathroom: a cheap plastic clamshell, just some beachfront souvenir, and felt a rush of tenderness, thought, *Thank God, she's been to the ocean.*

*

Dear F,

I always think of you more around our birthday, but the summer I turned twenty, I couldn't stop thinking, *She'll have been dead for twenty years.* Something about the roundness of the number, the magnitude of two decades, some presumed arrival of my own adulthood, threw your absence into sharp relief. I dreamed about you every night for weeks. You were always faraway, across a river or a wide field, looking back at me with my own eyes. You were always still and sitting on the ground. You never came for me, or reached toward me, but you looked and looked. In the dreams, I always had to be the one to walk away and leave you.

*

Dear F,

You come to me at the strangest times. It isn't always my face that does it, although that's an easy trigger. More often, actually, it happens when I am putting on my shoes and my eye catches on the slight, pale plank of my foot, or when I am calling to someone across a great distance and I hear my own voice ringing in the air. A man brings my hand slowly to his mouth, kisses the heel of my palm. My first thought: *This could be your hand.* And then: *You'll never have a lover.*

*

Dear F,

I wonder how often our mother looks at me and misses you.

*

Dear F,

We were born too early to have ever opened our eyes. I just realized that means we never saw each other.

*

Dear F,

I hope you weren't afraid.

World Maps

Lillian-Yvonne Bertram

1990

The first McDonald's: opens in Moscow

Reunification: of Germany

Foundation: of the World Wide Web

The Bills:

Buffalo Savings Bank: dissolves

Superbowls lose their first of four

Nelson Mandela: released from prison

O R E O

I lurk by the door
overhear
Ma explain the
n word
to my brother
he was the first
to hear it
in the third
grade

I play pretend
that I am
Macaulay Culkin,
a famous white
beloved
by all

1993

Get out of my way **BITCH!** *I'll hit you in the face with this basketball!*

(She hits me in the face with the basketball.)

She was blockin me!
I told her to get out of my way and let me make a shot!

(But that's the game. It's basketball.)

Whatever bitch. High yellow **BITCH.**

(Wait but—)

Good hair miss high yella black America **BITCH.**

Well you ACT white

No but **what are you** really

Only **white** people eat cheese like that

pulling it apart into strings

That's how white **people** eat

touching their food all over

Which is the white one?

Your mama or your daddy?

Why did you cut all your hair off when you had such **GOOD** hair!

You could have given it to **ME**

instead of wasting it.

1994

*Are you a **DYKE**?*

(Seventh grade. I don't know
what a dyke is.)

*You know—like **DYKE, BUTCH,
LESBIAN.***

*(She's rolling her eyes. It's art class
and we are making personality
collages.)*

(Mama says my African
hair is the hair that
curls and kinks and
won't lie flat.)

(Mama's friend said
that by straightening
my hair, I was setting
us all back.)

(Back to where?)

*But what **are** you?*

*Oh you're **black**?*

More like cream with some coffee.

I thought you was Dominican.

Latina.

I swear to god you was Egyptian. I can tell.

Libyan. All the way.

*Where do you get your **color** from?*

*I know you ain't **white**.*

*Why you have a picture of
two girls kissing then?*

(I don't know.)

I jus' liked it. It's a nice picture.

Oh. Well. You cut your hair off is all.

*And you had the **GOOD** hair too.*

(Are you a dyke?) I collage over the girls kissing.)
(Cover them with a **PIANO**.)

You're not, like,
really black.
You're more like
                  one of us.

                        We want
                        a picture of you
in our brochure.

1998

At the bookstore
pretending to look
anywhere other
than the cover

At the bookstore
pretending to look
anywhere other
than the cover
of *Female Masculinity*
looking back
wearing a form
of my own
face
buy *Pretty in Punk*
& keep looking

JudoFire999: H
Me: Hi
JudoFire999: H
Me: Fine, u?
JudoFire999: nig

JakeRock69: Hi
Me: Hi
JakeRock69: how old are u
Me:
Me: 13
JakeRock69: wanna suck dick

(every time it airs
I watch
The Incredibly True Adventure

of Two Girls

In Love

volume low,

last-channel button at the ready
set to NICK
or DISC
just in case my mom or dad
walks in)

The Little Girl, Her Drunk Bastard Parents, and the Hummingbird

Jessica Lind Peterson

A little girl with reddish brownish hair and big feet sat in a treehouse in her backyard. The treehouse was situated on the ground next to the garage, not up in a tree like you were thinking, and the treehouse was made of wood from the rotting back porch as the little girl's father was a railroad worker, and railroad workers do not have special access to wood scraps like construction workers do. Also notable, the treehouse had no roof and no walls, which made things sunny and fresh-smelling like dirt and apple blossoms and leaves and garages. The no roof/no walls detail will come in handy during the part where I tell you that a hummingbird flies into the treehouse, because if I told you that a hummingbird flies into a treehouse that *did* have a roof/walls you might think the hummingbird would have died on impact. I'm only trying to save you from despair.

In the little girl's hands was a round piece of wood which held a white piece of cloth which held a cross-stitch pattern of bright summer flowers which was very pretty indeed, though the stems on the flowers were a little bit crooked but so was the floor of the treehouse and that certainly may have had something to do with it. The little girl was briefly paused in her work because she felt like something was missing in her pretty scene of crooked flowers and so she needed to think about it. She always thought best when she was in her treehouse so this was all very convenient. And speaking of conveniences, the thinking break came at a good time because the needle had caused a major indent on the end of her right index finger and she had put it in her mouth to soothe it. Let's just call it what it was: a sewing injury. (Her grandmother had told her this might happen. Her grandmother cross-stitched and also baked bread that the little girl was very fond of. Sometimes, she ate a whole half of a loaf right out of the oven with butter and raspberry jam and it ruined her dinner, but her grandmother let her and that is why this grandmother was her very favorite grandmother out of all her grandmothers. Also, the other grandmother always made the little girl sit in her great big lap and pluck the wiry black hairs from her chin with a tweezers. Gross, but also a nice challenge on Sundays. There was love there but a favorite grandmother is a favorite grandmother and no one on planet earth can argue with that kind of sound logic. Her favorite grandmother was especially important these days since her father was a drunk bastard and her mother was on her way to becoming a drunk bastard. These are strong words but these are strong times. At first, it was just wine. Lots and lots of red wine. Her grandmother came to stay for two weeks and discovered a gargantuan amount of wine bottles in the recycling bin and also two opened bottles in the unused basement sauna under an old ten-gallon paint bucket. After her grandmother confronted her mother about all those wine bottles two things happened. One, the mother began putting empty wine bottles into the neighbor's recycling bins very early in the morning on the day of recycling pickup. Two, the mother began drinking seven sevens with Canadian Club because it worked faster and that is what the drunk bastard father drank and Canada is not far away so it's good to support our border friends. If the grandmother said anything about the whiskey bottles the mother could just blame the father, badda bing, badda bang. It actually worked because even though the little girl told her grandmother that the mother was still doing weird, drunk bastard-type things like burning her arm so badly while taking a roast out of the oven that the fabric from her Christmas sweater actually became scorched into her skin like a tattoo, hiding her glass of booze behind picture frames in the early afternoons, talking to the little girl, who was thirty-eight years old, in a baby voice as if she were a toddler and also forgetting her birthday all the time—her grandmother dismissed it, saying that perhaps the mother didn't want to get rings on the important parts of the coffee table and she was just being considerate of the furniture.)

Just so we're clear here. Two drunk bastard parents, one nice grandmother who is good at baking.

The little girl sat on the hard wooden floor of the treehouse sucking on her sore finger thinking about fresh bread and what else might go into her scene of crooked summer flowers and you'll never guess what happened next. The little girl started drinking whiskey too because fuck it, she liked the way it burned her throat just the right way and life was sad and hard and her husband had made a mistake exactly two years prior and she was having a difficult time with forgiveness and one or two drinks at night didn't mean she was turning into a drunk bastard for crying out loud it's not like she's going to put a gun to her head while standing on the shores of Lake Superior in the middle of the afternoon in front of a pastor and his wife celebrating their wedding anniversary like her pretty, drunk aunt with a developing interest in crystals who was only fifty years old had just done. Gawd.

Anyway. A hummingbird flew right into the treehouse and landed on the uneven wooden floor in a small, feathery thump. A thump so quiet, it barely registered on any super secret seismic sound scale that was or was not recording backyard sound waves in that particular part of the Midwest. So quiet, it could have been a damp dandelion puff. Or a snip of overgrown bangs floating to the floor. Or a large ladybug landing. The little girl picked up the hummingbird and held it very carefully in her hand (the one without the gruesome sewing injury) and the first thing she thought was that this hummingbird was certainly a goner. One translucent wing motored hopelessly against her palm, the other one was tucked and still against its feathered thumb of breast. Its tongue, a lolling pink string, hung from the end of its needle beak. So tired and such a goner was this hummingbird, that it could not even reel its own tongue back in. Sad, but understandable. Circumstances were dire.

The little girl knew she should carry the hummingbird outside, set it in the grass and walk away, but that is not what she did. She just couldn't. She had a real dying fairy on her hands and she wanted to keep looking. The hummingbird glowed in the sunlight, green and red and neon, a tiny shimmering flag of itself. Nothing had ever been sadder or more beautiful at the same time. Not even a wet horse. Not even an orphaned baby elephant. Not even old roses. The little girl began to cry because to not cry was impossible. She felt so bad for this hummingbird who was clearly dying. It should be whirring above the treehouse in blissful fits of motion. A mini, slick speed skater ripping through its track of air, magic in its fastness. To hold it, the little girl knew, was wrong. But it did not belong on the ground either. What would a hummingbird do with a sidewalk? Or sidewalk chalk for that matter? And she didn't want to put something so fragile as a one-winged hummingbird in the path of a drunk bastard mother who trips and falls on sidewalks and bruises three ribs while babysitting her three-year-old grandson. Uh huh. No way. She did not want that on her reddish-brownish head.

The little girl decided that continuing to sit there in the treehouse while holding the hummingbird in her non-injured hand seemed like the best plan for now. Though that plan faintly resembled doing nothing, she wasn't going to beat herself up about it. She was comfortable holding birds. Always had been. When she was an even littler girl, she had a pet parakeet named Blinkie who was blue and white and blinked alot in accordance with his name. Every day after school the little girl would engage in intense training sessions with Blinkie. First, she taught him to fly directly from his cage to her finger. Then, she taught him to crawl from her finger all the way up to her shoulder. Then, she taught him to sleep on her bedpost at night. She loved Blinkie and Blinkie did or did not love her back. It's tough to tell with pet birds. They have that bird look, like, I'm just looking at you to gather some information here. I like birdseed. Sitting on your finger is fine. Just keep the fucking golden retriever in the living room and I'll be your little friend.

It was a relationship that just *worked*.

The one thing the little girl could never get Blinkie to do was talk. It's not that she didn't like his sweet garbly goos. She totally did. But she longed for some real conversation. Some actual words. Some tête-à-tête. So she bought a record at the Goodwill called *Teach Your Parrot to Talk* and played it every day after school, sometimes over and over again. Here is an example of what the record sounded like:

Hello. Hello.

(Next track.)

Pretty bird. Pretty bird.

Poor Blinkie never picked up talking most likely because he was not a parrot. Parrots are smarter and have better mouth muscles. Meanwhile, the little girl played the record so many times and with such fervor it began to skip and skip and then, one day, it mysteriously disappeared.

Just like Blinkie.

When the little girl left for school one morning, Blinkie was there.

When she came home from school in the afternoon, Blinkie was gone. His cage was on the front porch and the drunk bastard mother said with a confused but semi-happy look on her face, *I went to change his water and he must have snuck out and flew away. Oh well. Too bad so sad. We can get another parakeet.* It was strange that the mother put the cage outside in the first place. Strange that the water needed changing, as the little girl always kept it fresh. Strange that Blinkie would have jumped through the water slot which was a space barely big enough for him to squeeze through. All of it was strange but when your mother tells you a story and you are a little girl those end up being the facts. Also in the fact pile is the fact that the little girl never trimmed Blinkie's wings because she wanted him to feel very alive even though he lived in a dining room and not the jungle. Now he was alive and gone.

The little girl went into action. First, she spread a white sheet out over the front lawn. Then, she sprinkled bird seed all over the sheet. Then, she put on her jelly shoes and circled the neighborhood block by block, scanning trees and roofs for blue movement until it became too dark for seeing small birds. Nothing. Not even one garbly goo. Her big feet were blistered from blanketing the neighborhood in bad footwear so she went home, sat in the living room recliner, and used an entire box of Kleenex to mop up the wet mess that poured out of her little girl face. This was the saddest thing that had ever happened. Sadder than dinosaur bones not being believed. Sadder than rain.

Blinkie the finger lander. Blinkie the shoulder rider. Blinkie the bed fellow. He was gone and would probably starve to death or get eaten by some damn golden retriever.

Back in the treehouse, the little girl put Blinkie out of her mind and instead, re-focused on the current sad bird story of her life. Since she was going to be in the treehouse for a while with the dying humming-bird, she settled in, resting her head against the wall that wasn't there and stretching out her long legs slowly like melancholy. The weather, at least, was nice. It was doing what weather did and she felt relaxed by it. Air moved through the treehouse in a soft, quiet way. The sun thought-fully warmed little girls and creatures everywhere, whether recovering from major sewing injuries or simply dying. The hummingbird shut its tiny black eyes and stopped trying to fly somewhere for once.

Time painted slow shadows across the lawn. The sun or the earth moved a little, she could never remember which one did what. There are just so many things to understand and a person has to prioritize. The little girl couldn't take the hummingbird inside the house. Too risky. There was a springer spaniel named Sparky in the living room and a turtle with no name living in the bathroom. And she didn't want to leave the hummingbird alone in the treehouse. What if it was confused by its surroundings? What if it died all alone? The little girl wondered what her favorite grandmother would say about all of this. Probably something that started with,

Oh Honey.

And then she'd pause.

And then she'd say,

Well . . .

And then she'd look at the little girl.

And the little girl would look at her.

And then, at last, after the appropriate amount of pausing and thinking, the favorite grandmother would slide a plate of day-old muffins or banana bread in front of the little girl and mention something about letting go of things that are beyond our control. Things like lost or dying birds, or forgotten birthdays, or scars that resembled tattoos. She would not mention all the crazy shit that she herself had let go of. Like when the little girl's mother discovered her father's Cadillac parked at a motel in the middle of the day and knocked on the door to find out why he was parked at a motel in the middle of the day and the answer was that he was making a major mistake with a woman he had met at the ski lodge. She would not mention any of that. She would also certainly not mention Jesus or chores which was another reason this grandmother was her favorite grandmother.

Feeling reassured by all this hypothetical grandmother advice, the little girl picked up her cross-stitch scene of pretty crooked flowers and wondered if they might straighten toward the sun over time, like real flowers. Wondered if maybe she should just let them be. Maybe nothing at all was missing here and she should just get a grip. The hummingbird turned in her hand and opened one tiny eye, surprising her like a sinkhole. It was panting now and making small wheezing noises. Picture an ant playing an ant-sized accordion. That was the small and woeful song of the dying hummingbird.

A sudden urge to be heroic overtook the little girl and she felt a crackling inside her chest like she had swallowed a sparkler. She wanted to save everything. To believe everything could be saved. But saving the hummingbird was out of the question, things were too far gone and she was no veterinarian. Just a little girl with a sewing injury who really really liked bread. All she had was what she had. And so, the little girl set the cross-stitching down in her lap, lifted the broken hummingbird with its lolling string of tongue close to her mouth and whispered, *What if we both just lay here, and pretended we were mysterious?*

As If to Say

Michael Torres

AMERICAN DREAM

In the United States a man can make a profit fixing used cars and flipping them. My father fills his driveway with vehicles. Parks them in the street. "Five cars at one time," he tells my mother in Spanish. "Can you believe it—a poor boy from Mexico with all this?"

BREAKFAST

Step 1: Sit next to your father at the table.

Step 2: Pour milk into a bowl of cinnamon Life.

Step 3: Position the cereal box between the two of you.

Step 4: Read the back panel.

Step 5: Repeat Step 4 until he leaves the table.

CONSTITUTION

My father memorizes the Preamble to the Constitution for his naturalization interview. He records himself reading it on a cassette tape: "We, the people of the United States, in order to form a more perfect union . . ." He plays it back, studies his voice.

Before leaving Mexico, my father worked on his grandfather's ranch, but the opportunities he was hearing about in the North seemed too great to pass up. At nineteen he decided to cross the border for the first time.

My father learned English from John Wayne movies. Now he listens to his own voice on the tape recorder. He rewinds and records it again, trying to sound more American.

DEGREES OF SEPARATION

If I need to ask my father a question, I ask my mother. I've always done this, to get around the fact that he and I hardly speak. It's not that we have nothing to say. We just don't know how to say it. He doesn't speak English very well, and I don't speak Spanish very well, so neither of us is even going to try. We talk through my mother. She is the only one in the family who really knows him.

All I have learned about my father's childhood has come from her. Here is a story she told me: My father had never seen a bicycle until the day his friend rode up on one. The boy taught my father how to find his balance, how to ride. The boy wanted the bike back, but my father wouldn't stop pedaling around the ranch, and the boy finally left. The next day the boy retrieved his bike. So my father decided to make his own bike from wood. For days he gathered scrap lumber and worked on it, a hammer in his hand, nails in his mouth. He built as much as he could but was unable to finish it. There was no way for him to construct a wooden chain, to get the gears to turn.

ENGLISH

My father wants his four American-born children to speak to him in English so he will learn the language better. He thinks he'll find more job opportunities this way. My first-generation Mexican American mother speaks perfect English *and* Spanish. Her family owned a ranch in Southern California. She went to charm school. She's not dark skinned. She helps my father navigate his double life as a Mexican and an aspiring American.

FIGHT

I'm fifteen when I come home with a black eye. I hang my backpack on a chair and yell, "I'm home!" A moment passes; then my father yells, "OK!" He says my mother and sister are at the store. Our conversations are like this: short and in English. I call to him again, asking if I can borrow his car so I can go see a girl. He enters the kitchen with the keys and sees my eye. I wonder if he'll be mad, but he doesn't say anything. He just winces. I want him to ask how it happened, but he doesn't. He stares at me as if it hurts him, too. Does this make me happy? He drops the keys in my hand and asks if I need money. He presses a twenty to my palm, his way of showing love.

GETTING HOME

My father starts the car after the swap meet and says, "I don't know how to get home." I'm only eight. He wants to know if I can find my way back without him. I sit up and look over the dashboard. My father keeps his foot on the brake, waiting. "Go straight," I say. He drives straight.

For the next fifteen minutes I direct him to turn left and right. He is pretending to be lost, claiming a sudden case of "amnesia." I begin to wonder if he knows who I am. Somehow it is easier for us to speak to each other like this. "Turn," I say, watching the road. "It's that way."

HIJOS (SONS)

In my early twenties I tell a friend that I don't talk to my father much. She says it's because I don't speak Spanish. This friend doesn't let her sons speak English at home. All day they speak English at school. At home she insists they use Spanish. If her kids don't speak Spanish, she says, how will they talk to their grandparents, learn their stories and history?

IDIOMS

In the rare conversations I had with my father growing up, he used American sayings he'd picked up. On Sundays, heading out for the swap meet, he'd say to me: "You ready, Freddy? Let's get this show on the road." To him, being an American was like being an actor: you just had to learn your lines.

JAULA DE ORO (GOLD CAGE)

There's a song by the band Los Tigres del Norte that includes a bilingual exchange between an undocumented immigrant and his Americanized son. The father in the song can neither forget nor return to his homeland, and because he fears deportation, he hardly ever ventures out in public. The United States for him is a gold cage. He asks his son, in Spanish, if he would like to go back to Mexico: "Escúchame, hijo. ¿Te gustaría que regresáramos a vivir a México?" The son answers in English: "I don't want to go back to Mexico. No way, Dad."

KITE

I'm ten and looking through the window at the neighborhood boys, who are talking to my father. I know they are speaking Spanish because he is smiling. The language must sound like home to him, like his village, Yahualica, a place I have never been and whose name I can barely pronounce. I picture a dirt road, a wooden bicycle. The boys want to fly the kite my father has made for me. I hate those boys for the access they have to him. Spanish is the key that unlocks the door to my father.

LENGUA (TONGUE)

My tongue is uncomfortable with Spanish. I speak it slowly and carefully, if at all, certain I will use the incorrect verb conjugation. I fear native Spanish speakers will wonder who I am, where I belong.

There is a video of me speaking Spanish on my fourth birthday. Just one word, but it's there, clear and confident, as if even my thoughts were in Spanish: My extended family—*primos, tios, y tias*; cousins, uncles, and aunts—have gathered under the shade trees in our front yard. My father is performing his favorite party trick, roping my older brother with a lasso. Then my brother walks out of the frame, and I cross my father's path. He swings the lasso above his head, throws it over me, and pulls me toward him. Angry, I shrug off his rope, toss it to the ground in front of him, and yell, "¡Tu!"—*you*. But that's incorrect. Watching the recording,

I shake my head at my younger self. I should've used the formal *usted*, as a gesture of respect.

On screen I run away. Again my father swings the lasso over his head and lets it fly.

MACHOS (MALES)

My best friend's uncles live next door. These macho undocumented Mexican men talk to my father from their side of the fence. If I go outside and say, "Hi," they demand I say it in Spanish: "¡En Español!" These men tower over me and bend down to speak with their Marlboro breath. I never reply to them in Spanish, but my father doesn't yell at me for this. He just laughs. My father won't speak to me in English—not in front of the neighbors. Still, he is proud to have produced a son who can fully embrace an American identity. At the age of eight I am cocky, brazen. I stick my tongue out at the neighbors when they ask for Spanish. I am an extension of my father's American Dream. At the same time, he cannot fully embrace his own Americanness, because he's afraid he will forget where he came from. And he cannot do that, especially not in front of these men. He remains loyal to his Mexican identity. Ultimately our loyalties will begin to divide us.

Perhaps my father didn't realize he was raising a son who would become a contradiction to him: A son who is both Mexican and American. A brown boy with a Spanish last name and English pouring from his mouth.

NATURALIZATION

The parents of the woman I am dating have some cement in their yard that needs to be broken up. I offer to help. They are naturalized American citizens originally from Mexico, and they like their daughter's suitors to be Spanish speaking, college bound, and *con respeto*—respectful. I bring my gloves and shovel, a cap to keep the sun off. I prove my worth through my work. I have a lunch bag with almonds and a frozen bottle of water. I swing a sledgehammer through the California summer morning and stay until the job's done. When my girlfriend's mother speaks to me in Spanish, I try to think of the Spanish words to reply, but I can't. I imagine she doesn't see me as a real Mexican. I'm a foreigner wherever I go.

Sometimes I wonder if my father ever stopped feeling foreign. When he first arrived in the United States, his job supervisors could not or would not call him by his name, Juan. Instead they called him Johnny: "Good morning, Johnny." And my father had to smile and say, "Hello," in his best John Wayne English.

I imagine my father getting ready for work. He buttons up a shirt with a name stitched to the chest, over his heart. A name that is not his.

OBSERVATION

When I move to Minnesota, no one I meet speaks Spanish. I should be relieved, but here my brown skin is loud. I learn that some white people pay good money to make their skin as dark as mine. I learn a dead deer in a truck bed can be a rite of passage for a boy. I've never felt as Mexican as I do just standing at the gas station in Minnesota, filling up my tank. It would take me twenty-six hours, driving southwest, to get home to Southern California.

PURSUIT OF HAPPINESS

Be a go-getter, but don't get caught up in the moment. Keep that poker face and play it by ear. If you're last but not least, you can work your way up. Little by little. It's all in a day's work. Actions speak louder than words. When opportunity knocks, reach for the stars on the other side of the tracks, where the grass is greener. In the home of the brave. Where the ramparts we watched were so gallantly streaming. If you can't beat 'em, join 'em.

QUESTIONNAIRE

Who is the father of this country? Name one of the two longest rivers in the United States. Where do you work? What does "We the People" mean to you? Name one state that borders Mexico. Name one problem that led to the Civil War. Who are your friends laughing on the other side of the fence? What time is your son coming home?

RESULTS

My father passed his citizenship test. He prepared by memorizing the answers to common questions, so he could pretend to speak English during the interview. Perhaps my father and I are not so different. I've been in school all my life: taking tests, collecting degrees, refining that résumé, pretending to speak Spanish and sometimes, with a lot of luck, succeeding.

SKIN

When my father decided to leave his grandfather's Mexican ranch to pursue a better life in the United States, he waited three months. Three months, he figured, is how long it would take for the calluses on his palms to heal; for his skin, out of the sun, to lighten. He knew he could get through the border patrol on a seventy-two-hour visitor's pass with his hazel eyes and smooth hands and light complexion.

TORRES

The first time a publication arrived in the mail with a poem of mine in it, my mother said my father pointed to our last name on the back cover and smiled at her as if to say, *I told you so.*

UNDOCUMENTED

For many years I didn't know my father was deported multiple times and had to cross the border again and again before he finally got a green card and lived here long enough to become a citizen. The only story I knew was of his arrival and the realization of his dream: a house and car for his family, a large front yard for his kids to run around in. Now I know that he worked in cotton fields and factories at first, places that could pay him under the table. I know that for a while he wrote the name of my mother's high school on job applications that asked about his education. (It was easier to get away with this back then.) When Mom said, "But you didn't go there," my father would laugh and say, "Technically, I did *go* there"—meaning, to talk to her.

In the summer of 2005 I took a job as a gardener, mowing lawns and raking leaves with my best friend's father and uncles. These men were Mexicans who had entered the United States without legal papers, men who never took their eyes off the road, who always drove the speed limit. They worked from early morning until all the houses and businesses they'd been assigned that day were done. I worked by their side in triple-digit heat because Curtis, our boss, reasoned, "If the mailman can work, so can you." Each day I'd come home more sunburned. In the shower I ached as I watched dirt swirl down the drain. I was nineteen, the same age my father was when he first crossed the border.

The day I started the gardening job, I wanted to prove I could endure, and I made the mistake of bringing only a bottle of water for lunch. At noon, when I had nothing to eat, my best friend's father, José, offered me his cup of tapioca pudding. I shook my head. He smiled and lifted the cup to me again. I took it, said, "Gracias," and slurped it down. I never failed to bring a full lunch again.

In the fall I left to attend community college. My courses were planned out. Curtis said I could come back anytime.

A few years later Immigration picked up José. Within a week a new worker had arrived to take his place: drive the truck, sculpt the rose-bushes, and shape an elephant from a client's overgrown hedge.

VERIFICATION

I consulted spanishdictionary.com to check some of the Spanish words in this essay. I won't tell you how many times.

WALLS, TYPES OF

Language. Machismo. Border fences. Silence.

X

When I first dreamed of being a writer, I chose the pen name Michael de la Torre. I thought de la Torre projected power and a European heritage. I practiced writing it in cursive. I imagined signing documents, contracts.

Y

Spanish for *and*. A connecting of what might otherwise remain separated. *Tu y yo*. You and I.

ZACATE (GRASS)

When I remember my father at his happiest, he is watering the grass: his thumb over the end of the hose, spraying the front lawn in a slow back-and-forth motion, his other hand in his pocket. He scans the street, watches each car that goes by. Is this—his house, his cars, his American-born son, his well-maintained lawn—what he dreamed of? Or is he thinking of what he lost, what he can't go back to?

Perhaps this is actually the memory of when I was happiest.

My soccer ball thuds against the wall in the front yard. I could be seven or eight. I kick the ball closer to him, stop it under my foot, exaggerate my breathing. He takes his thumb from the hose. I don't need to say anything. In this moment we are un *papá y su hijo*: a father and his son. I turn my head to the hose and drink.

Signatures

Lyzette Wanzer

Michel Foucault must have been rolling in his grave. That, or he was winking. The order of things? A dark-skinned black bartender, old enough to be my grandfather, glasses, mustache, stately carriage, appeared in the parlor and inquired about our drink selections. Camille ordered a Cabernet; I declined. Puzzled, she asked, "Isn't Zinfandel your favorite?" and ordered a glass for me. I wouldn't make eye contact with the bartender. What must he think? What must he have endured over the decades, suffered, borne, to have matters come to this, to *this*, serving a black woman less than half his age in a tony parlor? This was, decidedly, a patent *dis*order of things. Helter-skelter, topsy-turvy, downside up.

~

One Cab, one Zin. Clear view of the curving staircase with gleaming bannister. The sofas, plush as mittens. Queen Anne graced everything else. A neat array of hors d'oeuvres on a three-tiered carousel. Camille helped herself to a small saucer of cucumber-and-cream-cheese squares. Whole wheat.

~

Beyond the introductory remarks on the landing page, the website had been inaccessible. All of the whitebready cargo tucked away behind a Members Only log-on screen. The intro said the club had been founded a century ago, and had a true country counterpart in the north Georgia mountains. Robert T. Jones Jr. golf course, stables, tennis, six-lane pool. The deep end, fifteen feet.

~

Drinks only, Camille insisted, just try it for drinks. We don't have to eat there. They don't do cash or plastic, we'll charge my husband's account. It'll be good literary fodder, don't you think, you might use it in a story sometime. Just want you to experience it. This was Atlanta, chocolate city extraordinaire, and she was still color-blind. Now, some would call that sort of vitiated vision progress, but not I. My preference? That folks see the import, see the impact, the implication of the questions they ask, the overtures they make.

~

She toured me around the club's five floors, wine glasses in our hands. I was most struck by the chess and billiard rooms, framed photos against dark-paneled walls showing row upon row of sartorial white males, rolls of prior chess teams in tight script, wizened parchment under glass. Camille pointed out some names with whom or from whom her husband's family connected, descended. On the top floor, the predominately Vietnamese American staff prepared a lavish ballroom for a wedding reception. Every staff member we encountered throughout greeted Camille by name.

~

Still, privilege implies, often confers, a genuine inability to step inside another's skin, to borrow perspectives. We had dinner reservations at the home-cooking restaurant, west end of town. I'd chosen it because I loved fried catfish. Camille liked it, too, but called midweek to say that, when we met on Friday, she'd like us to start off at her club. She kept meaning to ask me, but it always slipped her mind, etc. Located near the downtown hub, I'd passed by or under it numerous times, an austere brick edifice, white columns flanking the double-door entrance, large balcony set with round linen-covered tables, chairs, sometimes a polished piano, Rach concerto. I met her on the club's corner in cream chenille, *en garde*, rinsed in dread.

~

We returned our glasses to the bar. This time, I endeavored to make eye contact with the bartender, but he would not look at either of us. He took our glasses, one in each hand, an ounce of dignity for every heartbeat. My own beating so hard I could feel pressure behind my eyes, but he would not look, would not look. I was only a *guest* here; I didn't want to *be* here, I was *invited*. Coerced, almost. I am here under duress. I am ordinary, common, simple. Stop chastening me.

~

"Ready to leave?" I was, and proceeded from the parlor through the entry at a smart pace, several steps ahead of her. On the sidewalk, headed to her car, we stopped when we heard music wafting from the balcony. Now on the far side of 6 p.m., the tables filled with accoutered diners, a pianist and singer at the far end, ready to begin their set. A waiter in a white jacket saw us below, on the walkway, gestured behind him, both arms toward the tables, the question clear on his face. So appealing and earnest, we both laughed. Camille turned to me—"You're sure you won't try dining here? With the live jazz?"—and I relented. We retraced our steps back through the parlor. The Vietnamese maître d' met us at the balcony door, seated us, handed me the single-panel menu.

~

The white female singer looked to be mid-thirties, close-cropped coif, perched on the balcony rail, black spaghetti-strap dress, and the pianist, a seventy-five-year-old-year-old portly Italian native. Ought to be

interesting, I thought, and it turned out to be exactly that. A gentle-
man in crisp, unrelieved white, bow tie to shoes, moved from table to
table, clipboard in hand, taking song requests. Camille requested Anita
O'Day. I asked for "Love Me or Leave Me" and Billie Holiday's ren-
dition of "All of Me." The singer didn't know either. What sort of jazz
performer was she? I had no problem requesting either piece at any
number of jazz clubs in the city. Topsy-turvy, downside up, downside up.

~

I've become a good reader, know how to interpret body language, gestures, signals, looks, when the mouth says one thing and the body betrays
the lie. I met the eyes of diners at neighboring tables, seeking hostility,
dismay, suspicion. One woman grinned at me, supremely unexpected.
A man did too, but his smile, only half of him in it. Ginger-seared sole
was exquisite, spiced with melt-in-the-mouth, nuanced undertones.
The waitstaff was uber attentive. The chef herself came out, long hair
wrapped under a white net, addressed Camille as Mrs. Hartwick, asked
how the dishes were, and what did we think of the wine pairings? She
smelled of onions, peppercorn, curry.

~

After their first set, the duo took a break. The singer headed inside,
the venerable pianist, in full-bore tux, headed to our table and, in fact,
directly toward me. Inclined his head. I know "All of Me" and can play

133

it, but Lana did not have the lyrics memorized and so could not sing it. Quite insistent that he was conversant with the song, with Lady Day, with Lena Horne. Sicilian residue coated his syllables. His grave sincerity made me pat his hand. We smiled at each other. He closed his eyes and nodded. The bartender entered, presented a bottle of Pinot Blanc to the table beside ours, folded towel cradling the glass. The guests leaned, as though they were on a sloping deck, to scrutinize the label. He turned to look at me. Over the pianist's back, our gazes held.

~

Something is awry, given the humiliations, deprivations, constraints you've suffered; something is awry, so that I might even be able to enter this club; something is awry, off-kilter, about there being only we two here, in Atlanta, just us two, in a city *like* Atlanta, only we two here, just us two, and you serving me. Sir, I wanted you to know how that grabs me, that I've got my mind around that conundrum. Sir, I comprehend disorder. Grasp disarray. Recognize dissonance when I hear it. I don't have it twisted.

Toward a Poetics of Phantom Limb, Or All the Shadows That Carry Us

Jennifer S. Cheng

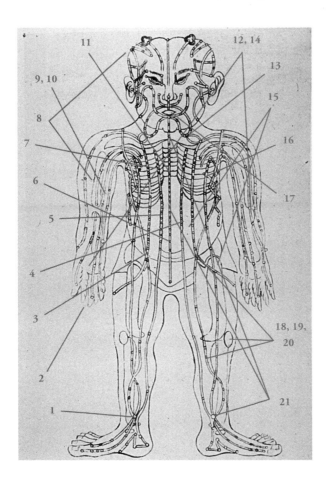

1. If I started out *Map of the Inner [Text]*, and what I really meant was *body as map*: body as inscribed with the pathways of our navigations: our hidden histories at hand. If by *hidden*, I meant *unconscious, lost, never known*.

2. Here is where the attachment we once knew as *body* begins to disappear, an erasure of time and friction. A palimpsest in waiting. You thought it was there, and then it evaporated. Or it wasn't there, but instead, pain. Every night I came across another description: *holloway, shul*. It was an excavation whose imprint held its own meaning or weight. Sometimes the emptiness is a footprint: *"a mark that remains after that which made it has passed by."* Sometimes it is a pathway: *"an impression in the ground left by the regular tread of feet."* And sometimes: *"the scarred hollow in the ground where a house once stood."*

3. This can apply to many things, but let us start here, the literal houses left behind in every generation of my family—first house, village house, narrow walk-up house, house near the sea, and so on. Where once a dwelling was meant to shelter the entire family, a wholeness of appendages, now it was scattered by chance and by force, it was abandoned and taken, it was forgotten or barely known. What does this do to the body and the knowledge it carries—sense of where it has been, how it moves through the world, its feeling of location? The answer is also the language with which it articulates itself: it holds a shadow space that is and is not. It learns a hollow as home, as body. A confession: at first I read *scarred* as *sacred*.

4. Instead, the dust and particles we may not otherwise notice. It was into my adult years when I realized that my mother had older brothers. Living ones, still across the ocean. I had never seen them or heard them mentioned, even when my family lived on that side of the globe. And yet I was not wholly surprised because how could I have known to name a ghost, an empty space, if it had always been part of the atmosphere? All of the families around us were like this. *We accepted the shadows we found ourselves in*, an author wrote. One of the brothers would eventually come to the U.S. and work in a toothpaste factory for less than minimum wage. *He can write beautiful essays in English but cannot speak it*, my mother would finally say. Later on he would stop speaking to her because once upon a time one was left behind a border and one was not. Every year my mother mailed him money and vitamins.

5. I could point to this boundary if I had to; it divides the body even as it scales it.

6. I map the ghosts; the ghosts map me. For I have written about the strange ambiguous homesickness I have known in the hollow cavity of my stomach every now and then since childhood. It comes out of nowhere and travels like an unwanted tingle through my nerves. I said *untethered, abstract and metaphysical*. I said, *for although as a child I was often homesick—at school, at the neighbor's house, anywhere unfamiliar or foreign—I also at times felt an inexplicable longing while inside my own house.*

7. If inside we were a web of invisible and tenuous material. *Knowledge that is missing* and yet *in the bones*. To try to locate the specifics of a general sense of haunting is like trying to remember a dream in the saturation of daylight; one suddenly recalls a feeling of weight without being able to place it. When I say that History is like a family member, I mean not dead but half-missing, or an intimacy half-strange and, let's say, half-asleep, like muted white noise. I can feel its movements inside me, a restlessness in my limbs, but what exactly *it is* I cannot say.

8. A slight receding of the page or all this negative space: as carrying heft.

9. Symptoms range from *tingling* and *itching* to *burning* and *aching*. Symptoms worsen with the weather.

10. One hypothesis for spectral phenomena of the body is that it is part of a *mourning process*. A mourning across time, then: this inheritance of ghosts.

11. [   ] as that which we do not know and still we know. Hastening through the veins. [   ] as where we store our truths, not as in secret but as in: [   ], *absorbed, quelled*. Storms we accepted into the space beneath our lungs, breathing out and in through a cloud as if it were normal; aches near the joining of arm and torso, which we took for granted. They become holes and [   ] I cannot name.

Alienated from one's own body, I [   ]. In the darkness, swatting
and grabbing at all the uncertain [   ].

12. If a body is a diagram that looks like it is exhaling in parts. That
is charting something invisible, the need for a shape to trace the
half-known. A poetics of absence might also encompass a poetics of
traces in exile, lost and abandoned particles of dirt and light. What
does it mean to translate a ghost over and over? What is the poetry
of the atmosphere inside a crater? *Scarred, sacred, scared.*

13. *Familiar; unfamiliar. Conscious; unconscious. Substance; absence.*

14. What can still be described: its posture, the feeling of it moving
around, the impact it has on the air and objects around it.

15. This, then, the small things we capture by accident, like a mislaid
dust-print or the cut-out of an old shadow. It travels throughout
our bloodstreams, our organs, our muscles and joints, and becomes
large though silent that way. But when did I finally know that my
father was one day reunited with his father and his siblings, after
he had left another home and began his own family? How much
did I know and not know when we all lived on the same side of the
world, eating our meals together amid the interaction of utensils,
bowls, plates, our many-languaged mouths? In lieu of memory, the
body transmits circulations of air by which we learn to move and
breathe. When I was twelve, my parents, not wanting to risk history

repeating itself, traveled ahead to the U.S. to look for a home for our family. I do not remember for how long I felt their absence, but the day they returned was the first time I learned one could cry not from sadness or physical pain but a shattering exhale that tells the body it has been holding its breath.

16. Someone said *home* and *body* and *history*, and that someone was me. Freud described the sensation of familiarity tiding toward unfamiliarity and vice versa: *home* and *un-home*. This, too, can apply to many strands of the immigrant body, threaded and intersected toward absented dimensions. If *home* is a body, and a *body* is a home, then what does it mean: *[an uncanny place]; [in the dismal night hours]; [ghastly; (of a house) haunted]*. Or later: *A familiar thing that has undergone repression and then emerged from it.*

17. All I can give are scant gestures, wholly inadequate. How much of history can we never really know except in this way? My brother, sister, and I grew up watching movies on our television with my parents. By movies, I mean, *in our language* and sometimes a dialect that required translation. Our eyes on an imagined world, and my father, ever our protector, translating and narrating its happenings into our intimate sounds. One that didn't require translation that we watched over and over: [活著] *To Live*. In it, bodies grow thin like skeletons, bodies are beaten, bodies pile. Our eyes on the screen, our lungs yet letting in air. In the room: *That was my childhood*—, a voice made of wooden dolls and landscape paintings and miniature ships.

Syllables loiter in the air, they wrap around you or are absorbed through the skin, and then silence, again—

18. *Indentations, hollows, marks, scars.*

19. In other words, *embodied space.* Or perhaps, *somatic memories.*

20. Here is a circle, a node, at this juncture. Here is another one. What does this have to do with poetics? I will say it again: *indentations, hollows, marks, scars.* They become containers—for what? *Debris* of dust, light, fragments of the cosmos. An obsession I cannot let go of: the absences and excavations we cannot name yet carry in the recesses of our bodies. A map we breathe in and out a thousand times as we make into the wayward of the world. In *Ghostly Matters,* the sociologist says *a way of knowing* and also, therefore, *a way of saying.*

21. *Which part?* I never did ask in response to those hanging syllables. It wasn't a direct representation, see? It's a contour of a shape, and how can I know what courses at its center? All I can do is circle this shadow over here, draw a line from this place to that one, trace this pathway of ether, air, sky.

Notes

Image source (public domain): https://collections.nlm.nih.gov/catalog/ nlm:nlmuid-101449285-img

References and quotations in certain sections are attributed to the following sources:

2, 18, 20: Rebecca Solnit, *A Field Guide to Getting Lost* (2005).

4: Junichiro Tanizaki, "In Praise of Shadows" (1933).

6: Jennifer S. Cheng, *House A* (2016).

16: Sigmund Freud, "The Uncanny" (1919).

17: Zhang Yi-Mou, 活著 *To Live*, film (1994).

20: Avery Gordon, *Ghostly Matters* (1997).

Whens

Chloe Garcia Roberts

Remember when one morning we were home alone and instead of letting me brush out the tangles in your hair you asked to brush mine? Because you were so small, I sat cross-legged on the floor. At first the weight was too unwieldy for your tiny fat hand, and the brushing was more like being beaten softly about the head. But after a few minutes you got the hang of it and found your rhythm, rowing the brush roughly down the length of my hair. Lifting your arm to the crown of my head, letting it drift down again, lifting your arm to the crown of my head, letting it drift down again. Then, behind the slow shushing of the brush, behind the curtain of hair hanging around my face, behind my eyes closed underneath, an other side opened: a hallway into a when of you brushing my hair when I was no longer able. I felt just under the skin of my body, strong and capable as a mother, another body, weak and older. A self faintly felt of what was to come not what was. I felt the weight of both of your hands, the baby, the woman, my responsibility, my caretaker all in unison for a breath (and I do not say moment, or second, because that implies a unit of linear time and this was not of that rubric but rather a transversal touching together of different times). I heard the sound of the brush, the sound of your breathing, the sound of the morning behind my eyelids, but in two places, two points on a life. Together, you and I, we had brushed open a *whens*.

The reason a certain moment can seem suspended from the stream has nothing in fact to do with the present in which it occurs, but is instead a result of the number of future instances that that exact moment is recalled, remembered, replayed. This phenomenon is actually just our future selves overthinking the happening in question, which in turn breaks down its structure, its constitution like worn cloth or hollowed stone. This is the reason why the noise of life can sometimes silence itself, thin itself, to one tenuous thought like a silvery tendon spanning two dense slabs of muscled darkness (also known as *the future* and *the past*). Some people refer to this clarity, this one-note knowing, as intuition, which is false, primarily because it does not come from within (in-tuition) but from without. It is not a product of what you are (i.e., what you have become) but of what you will become washing backward. *Whens* then is a term for the tunnel between, the backward runnel which allows simultaneity to draw together, to bridge, two distinct times. So in this case I will be in a bed, in morning light, silent under your brushing, thinking, thinking, thinking backward to that first time under your hand.

Eventually every life will prove the existence of innumerable tiny currents running like this one from the future to the past, even if they are largely undetectable and invisible, even if like lines of faint embossing they are easier felt than seen. And experience of this phenomenon, a face you remember loving before you saw it, for example, is a clue one could use to determine that in this way the true future lies. To experience a *whens* is proof we live in a river that runs all ways, always.

+ + +

I've always thought that the best birth story I've ever read is that part in *Huckleberry Finn* when departing his own bloody murder scene, he unfolds himself into a boat and drifts into a mist shot with voices from the shore, this one and the other. Because he was in two places at once and also neither one; because he was between the shores; because he was a bridge, or maybe better, he was becoming a bridge; because he was a *whens*.

At least this is how it was for me when I reached for you, when you came to me. Blind as a boat, floating on the currents of other voices, the waves of other's touch, the deeps of pain. When we were both listening for the other. When I was a body of water in which you were surfacing. When I was the sway, the stretch, the snap of molecules. And when from beneath you rose: *Una ola*, a wave. *Una ala*, a wing.

My own birth story, or the one that is not my mother's to tell, happened one afternoon several years ago in a blackout over the whole lower half of the city. I wanted to be home and foolishly decided to try to navigate the lightless hallways of my apartment building alone to get there. After climbing the stairs in muffled light from high and far-off windows, I opened the heavy fire door to my floor, taking a quick look

145

in the gray of what direction I needed to go. But when the door shut behind me, it shut so darkly it was as if it never existed. And when I stepped with fingers outstretched into the deepness, I was unmoored, eyeless. At first I refused to believe in my powerlessness and floundered forward. But with each step I lost myself a little more, feeling that strange vertigo particular to pitch-blackness when the borders of the body start to inflate, then reduce, then waver. When finally I realized I was unable to reach my home, and that I was also incapable of returning the way I had come, I began to cry for help. And after a few minutes someone silently opened their door behind me and an oar of sunlight cracked the dark. I found myself just a few steps from my own door, in a corner. I had been asking for help from a wall.

For the rest of my life, as long as I am, I am there. Pressing myself against the faceless unanswering wall of god when behind me a door opens, a slight wing of light. This was a *whens* also, though a different type. Not a bridge connecting two points but the surge under the span—the flood.

+   +   +

A decade ago I was driving with my mother across the country. As we drew closer to the Mississippi we began to hear on the radio that the river was swelling its banks and slowly spreading and cutting off all the passages back east. As we drove, we flew by empty houses next to the highway filled with dark water. Great mouthfuls were torn out of the countryside, and replacing that missing land was a waving stillness

146

whose rising was so incremental, so unstoppable, it was answered internally with an equally black spill of fear.

When we finally made it to the banks of the great river itself, wide as a small sea, we drove straight across its turgid waters on a vast suspended bridge. And just under the surface of that suspended moment of crossing, I carried another moment: when less than a day before in northern Minnesota, I myself had spanned the infant river at its clear source in Lake Itasca, so slight and slender I had put one foot on this shore and one foot on the other.

A flood is just a widening of the between that causes a spilling of what was carried into what had carried it; an eclipse of the holding by what was held. *Après moi le deluge*, the French king says. And what he means is that he is the first singing sign of a reversal of the order of the world (another definition of to flood). But of course, we all can say this. The key is the word *après*, which yes means after but also means below and, most importantly, beyond—the direction whose mercy we all float along.

This is the moment where I admit to you that I have discovered time travel to be possible. And that I was ultimately taught this by translating the pain of a ninth-century poet into English. To clarify, I do not mean that a body can move to a different time than the one they were born into, but rather that like a stitch one can gather not just all the shores the self has touched, but others that have been shown to you clearly enough that you may claim them rightly as your own.

Let me explain: we know the way fiction works is that the words cause certain chemicals in your brain to go through a mirroring dance without action that makes the rest of the brain feel as if what is read is happening to it. The way poetry works is similar, but instead of action it involves emotion. And this is where it gets a bit complicated, because emotion isn't mirrored or aped. Like light, it is perceived or it isn't. And if it is perceived or felt then it is original, inseparable from any other time that it is. So a man burning in grief can send an arrow of words forward in time, can, through centuries, touch, can prove that years are not opaque but translucent, and thus can let those words, like light, pass through. Perhaps this is why to write is to dissipate the gloom, dilute the viscosity of the dark, because sometime, somewhere, now, someone else is lightening you.

In the place of my childhood floods came like lightning, they were immediate, a flash, an issue, an opening of water in the desert, an apparition made real. The rivers there are born torrentially like gods, whole and fully formed. Once in the spring after the snowmelt, a friend and I went out to the arroyo to throw sticks into the whipfast current that had appeared overnight. Suddenly, for a reason I no longer know, I stripped down to my underwear and stepped into the rushing water. I remember being hypnotized by the speed as I walked into its center, the way its force hit me, enclosing me in its power. And then where I had been standing, smiling, feeling the insistent pushing of the water against my legs, I was under, I was spun, I was thrown, down, around, away from the air. Time moves quick as water when you are about to drown, your flailing, your ragged breaths just so many droplets forced to rush in tandem along. Greater force holds you now and, not playfully in the least, tightens its hold.

Then just as I went completely under, I was thrown against a bank, a thin outstretched arm of sand, and suddenly I was free. I walked back upstream to my friend crying on the shore and we went home. My mother made a fire, wrapped me in a blanket, and while I sat cross-legged staring silently through the flames back into the mouth of the water, she brushed my hair.

Transgender Day of Remembrance: A Found Essay

Torrey Peters

Compiled and arranged from the "Remarks" section of Transphobia vs. Transrespect research project (2014) "Trans Murder Monitoring results: TMM TDOR 2014 Update."

Brunete was beaten to death with a stick. The victim was shot by two men on a motorcycle in front of a motel. The victim was shot in the head. The suspected murderer is a former military police man. A neighbor heard the victim scream at night and saw two men walking out of the victim's room but could not remember their faces. The case is under investigation. The victim was found tied to a chair with multiple stab wounds in her abdomen. Police reported that the trans person was well known and admired and murdered by her lover with seven stabs. A fourteen-year-old trans person was found strangled. The victim was stabbed eight times. The victim was shot by a man on a motorbike. The victim was shot two times by two men on a motorbike. The victim was found in a lake. She was a Romani person. The body of the victim was found handcuffed. The body of the victim was found dismembered. The body of the victim was found handcuffed. The victim was a person of color. The undignified way her burned body was dumped in a trash bin indicates transgender hostility. Rosa was a person of color and of Indonesian descent. Police is investigating a possible hate crime. Police is investigating the crime as a possible homophobic hate crime. Alondra was a person of color. Police suspects that more than one person was involved in what they describe as a barbaric murder. The victim was slaughtered, beaten and stoned; the corpse was found half naked in a wasteland. The face of the victim was smashed by the client with a stone after having sexual intercourse. The victim's body was found with tied hands in plastic bag on the road. Investigations revealed that several cars had run over the corpse. Noe Lopez was attacked at a sex worker's place, forced into a vehicle by a group of armed men wearing bulletproof vests and balaclavas. Amnesty International see this murder in connection with a series of murders of sex workers in San Pedro Sula. The note in the newspaper reports that the homicide is the product of insecurity and violence lived in the city. Sanchez was on her way to a party dressed in a skirt, when she was attacked by two men who stabbed her to death. Belizean LGBT NGO UNIBAM called the murder a hate crime. Sanchez had been harassed and received death threats in the days leading to her murder. The victim was killed with an ax after having a dispute with a young man in a bar. Witnesses reported that the victim was verbally assaulted and later shot. The victim was set on fire by four persons and died from burn injuries in a hospital. Buxexa was a person of color. The body of the victim showed signs of torture. The police believe that the murder took place because the victim was a trans person. Strangers shot toward the victim's house, causing her death. According to a newspaper report the victim was tortured and beaten to death by a lawmaker and four of his assistants accusing the victim of theft of a mobile phone. The murder is described as a barbaric crime. The victim was dismembered and her face totally destroyed with a knife. The victim was killed by a fourteen-year-old minor. The police is investigating the crime as a possible hate crime as this is the second stabbing of a trans person within one month and under similar circumstances. The victim was beaten to death by a group of people and found hanged. The victim was a person of color. Raissa was shot six times in the head and thorax. The victim was using a public phone when she was shot to death with ten shots by two men on a motorbike. Denise was tortured with the peak of a bottle. The victim was stabbed eleven times. She was attacked by a man in a group of five men. The murderer claimed that the victim criticized him on the unimpressive sex they just had. He was angry and then beat her with a hardwood and stole her valuables. The victim was found wrapped in a black plastic bag. The NGO Red Umbrella reports that Sevda's murderer was her boyfriend, who fled to Serbia from where he called the police and confessed the murder. Police reports that the murder was the result of fights between trans people. "Alex," an eight-year-old child, moved six months ago to Rio de Janeiro to live with the father. The father has beaten the child to death to "teach him to behave like a man," as the child did belly dancing, wore female clothing, and loved dishwashing. Camila was executed with fifteen shots. CCTV footage shows how a trans sex worker is approached by a man sitting in a car and then shot from the inside of the car. The victim was stabbed to death and her personal belongings were stolen such as her laptop computer. The murderer is still unknown and the case is under investigation. The victim's body showed signs of torture. Andressa was attacked by several persons at a cemetery and stabbed fifteen times. Rose Maria was stabbed twelve times. The murder happened several weeks after the implementation of the so-called Anti-Gay-Bill in Uganda. Queen, a trans sex worker, has been attacked by a guy, whom her friends believe she met at a bar. During the attack she called her friends by phone saying "the guy is beating me, the guy is killing me." She was found later by her friends with severe wounds and signs of torture (cuts from a bottle on her body and in her anus). Queen was hospitalized and died several days later. Coco was a well-known drag queen. The victim's body was thrown to the street; allegedly the police saw the event and did not intervene. Vanessa received death threats before she was murdered. Paulete was executed with fifteen shots when she approached a client in a car at night. The murder was reported as homophobic hate murder. Dani was beaten in the face, before she was shot to death. Parts of the body of the victim have been found in different garbage bags at a cemetery. The skin of the torso was torn off. The suspect is a special force police officer, who wanted to pay less for a service and killed Jade Esmeralda inside his car when she didn't agree. Giovana was a person of color. The victim was found stabbed to death in her condominium unit. The victim was beaten to death by a group of people in the middle of a street at night. The victim was hit in the head. Giovanna was stabbed eleven times. The victim presented stabs all around the body. She was murdered by two clients in her own apartment due to an argument over the price for the sexual service. The victim's body showed signs of physical violence and was hit on the head. The victim's body showed multiple wounds on its body. The victim was stoned. Nicole was shot five times in the head. The victim was found stabbed four times and her body was burned. The victim was a person of color. The arrested suspect offended Jenifer and two other trans women who were sex workers. Later he returned with another man in a car and stabbed Jenifer to death. The victim was a person of color. She was shot by two men. The victim was found tied up and showed signs of torture, with her face burned on purpose. Marcia was executed with a shot in the head. The victim's body was found in a pit and showed signs of torture, plus a shot to the head. Other bodies were found in the pit. The victim was a person of color. The victim was found tied with multiple stab wounds and with her genitals exposed. The victim was a person of color. Shayara was found beaten to death with a stick on a hill in Rio de Janeiro in the morning. A news magazine reported that she provided sexual services to a policeman the night before. The victim was a person of color. She was found burned behind a garbage bin. The victim was a person of color. The victim was raped before she was beaten to death with a stick. The victim's body was beaten multiple times on the face. The suspected murderer strangled Kellen and threw her body into the swimming pool of the hotel. Makelly was found naked and with signs of hanging. Police is searching for a man who is chasing and killing trans persons. Two men in a car approached Dennysi and shot four times at her. Dafine was walking in the street with another trans person, when two men on a motorbike approached them and shot Dafine to death. They also tried to shoot the other trans person but failed. The victim was having a drink in a bar when two men on motorcycles passed by and shot her in the head. The victim was suffocated with a plastic bag. The victim's body was found with both hands and feet tied up. The victim was stabbed fifteen times. The victim's body was found in female underwear and, as a newspaper reports, "without eyes." Two other trans women in Detroit were shot within days of the murder inside Palmer Park. Geovana was stabbed six times. The victim was found inside her own apartment. The suspected murderer had an argument with Alexandra in the street and shot her in the back only steps away from her home. Karen was seriously injured and thrown out of a moving car by a client. Cris was shot four times by a man passing by in a car. The police affirm that the victim was raped before being killed. The victim was walking with another person and was stoned, causing her to die. The victim's body was found in her apartment. Her body presented eighteen stab wounds. Mahadevi was impaired and pushed out of a moving train by two adolescents. It seems that the aggressors harassed the victim, who tried to hide, but they killed her with a shotgun. Bili was standing with two other trans people near a bus stand when a man namely Raja started misbehaving with Bili and got annoyed and stabbed and injured her. Bili died in the hospital. The body of the victim was found floating in a creek. Bruna was shot by a man on a motorbike when talking with a client in front of a motel. A local LGBT NGO speculates that the motive could have been "transmisogyny."

Annotating the First Page of the First Navajo-English Dictionary[1]

Danielle Geller

'ąą', well (anticipation, as when a person approaches one as though to speak, but says nothing).[2]

'aa'adiniih, venereal disease.

'ąą 'ádoolnííł, it will be opened.[3]

'aa 'áhályáanii, body guard.

'aa 'ą'ii, magpie.[4]

'ąą 'ályaa, it was opened.[5]

1 The first, incomplete Navajo-English Dictionary was compiled in 1958 by Leon Wall, an official in the U.S. government's Bureau of Indian Affairs. Wall, who was in charge of a literacy program on the Navajo reservation, worked on the dictionary with William Morgan, a Navajo translator.

2 I could begin and end here. My mother was raised on the reservation, but she was never taught to speak her mother's language. There was a time when most words were better left unspoken. Still, I am drawn to the nasal vowels and slushy consonants, though I feel no hope of ever learning the language. It is one thing to play dress-up, to imitate pronunciations and understanding; it is another thing to think or dream or live in a language not your own.

3 In August 2015 I moved from Boston to Tucson to join an MFA program in creative writing. I applied to schools surrounding the Navajo reservation because I wanted to be closer to my mother's family. My plan: to take classes on rugweaving and the Navajo language (Diné Bizaad); to visit my family as often as I can. It will be opened: the door to the path we have lost.

4 Magpies are the one bird I have not seen on the reservation. Birds I *have* seen in my grandmother's backyard: Cliff Swallows, Inca Doves, Sharp-shinned Hawks, Western Bluebirds, Western Scrub Jays, Phainopeplas, Northern Flickers, Ravens, and other carrion birds.

5 It was opened: a PDF version of the Navajo-English Dictionary from the University

'ąą 'ályaa, bich'į̱', it was opened to them; they were invited.[6]

'a 'áán, hole in the ground; tunnel; cave; burrow.

'ąą 'át'é, it is open.[7]

'ąą 'át'éego, since it was open.[8]

'á'ádaat'éhígíí, the fundamentals, elements.[9]

'áádahojoost'įįd, they quit, backed out, desisted, surrendered.

'aa 'dahoost'įįd, t'óó, they gave up, surrendered.[10]

'aa dahwiinít'įįį', into court (a place where justice is judicially

of Northern Colorado. I wonder which librarian there decided to digitize it. Most government documents, after they are shipped to federal depositories around the country, languish on out-of-the-way shelves and collect decades of dust before being deaccessioned and destroyed. I have worked in these libraries—I know.

6 One of the reasons Navajo soldiers were recruited as code talkers during the Second World War was because there were no published dictionaries of their language at that time—and because the grammatical structure of the language was so different from English, German, and Japanese. They were invited to a world beyond the borders of the reservation. My mother always told me the only way to get off the Rez is to join the military or marry off.

7 One of the first typewriters that could adequately record the Navajo language was built for Robert Young, a linguist who also worked with William Morgan and published a more comprehensive dictionary and grammar guide (*The Navaho Language*) in 1972. In the 1970s, a Navajo font was released for the IBM Selectric, an electric typewriter, which would serve as the basis for a digital font on early computers.

8 Navajo fonts are now available for download in multiple typefaces: Times New Roman, Verdana, and Lucida Sans. Numbers and symbols turn into letters with diacritical marks, the left bracket "[" becoming a "ł," a voiceless alveolar lateral fricative. Forming the sound becomes harder than typing it. The jaw relaxes, but the tip of the tongue rises. A breath is released, not down the center of the tongue but past the sides, catching the wet and weight of the cheeks.

9 In a seminar class marrying creative nonfiction and science fiction, I am given a story by Brian Aldiss titled "Confluence." The story is told in a series of dictionary entries translating an alien language that meets at the confluence of sound and body movement, where over nine thousand named stances can significantly alter the meaning of a word. Part of the joy of the story is finding where these meanings diverge, like when JILY JIP TUP is defined as both "a thinking machine that develops a stammer" and "the action of pulling up the trousers while running uphill." Meaning is built through accumulation, the fundamental elements of an alien culture—its language, norms, values, and artifacts—revealing themselves through repetition and relevance.

10 There are many reasons parents did not teach their children the Navajo language: U.S. monolingual policies, violence experienced in boarding schools, and perceived status. Many parents believed they were helping their children find their way into an English-speaking world.

administered).[11]

'áádéé', from there (a remote place).

'aadéé', from there.

'aa deet'á̧, transfer (of property, or ownership).[12]

'áádeisi̧i̧d, they discontinued, stopped, or ended it.

'aadi, there.

'áadi, there, over there (a remote place).[13]

'áádi̧i̧ł, it is progressively dwindling away; disappearing.[14]

'áadiísh, there? thereat?[15]

'a̧a̧ dinéest'á̧, they increased, multiplied. ('a̧a̧ has the meaning of extension or spread.)

'aadóó, from there.

'áádóó, from there on; and then; and; from that point on; from there.

Shash yiyiisxi̧ 'áádóó shí níseł'ah. He killed the bear and I skinned it.

11 September 13, 2015. My cousin-sister is scheduled to testify in court in one week; she isn't sure if she wants to go. I pick her up anyway. Bring her back to Tucson with me.

12 My aunt tells me we have land on the reservation, just off I-40. We've inherited it from our great-grandmother, Pauline Tom. Only, Pauline Tom had many children, and their children had many children, and after she died in 2008, all those children started fighting. It's a common problem, and it isn't unique to the Navajo Nation. Federal land allotment policies have resulted in too many heirs for too few acres.

13 September 13. On the drive to Tucson along I-40, my cousin-sister points out the black-tar roofs of our family's houses. She tells me our relatives in Sanders called her Dibé Yázhí, Little Sheep, after the animals our great-grandmother raised. She points out the cemetery—a small, square piece of land—where our grandmother is buried. The cemetery is barely distinguishable from the rest of the landscape, and when I follow my gaze, look away from the highway, I see only the stark, white faces of the headstones and the silver glint of a ribbon in the wind.

14 In 1968, a decade after the first Navajo-English Dictionary was published, 90 percent of the children on the reservation who entered school spoke Navajo; in 2009, only 30 percent knew the language (Bernard Spolsky, "Language Management for Endangered Languages: The Case of Navajo," *Language Documentation and Description 6* [2009]: 117).

15 September 22. The second time I pass our allotment on I-40 a week later, I try to find the spot Dibé Yázhí showed me. I look for the headstones; I think of stopping and trying to find my grandmother's grave. My cousin-sister told me that if you don't do the proper blessing, the spirit will follow you home. (She asked me, "What is the difference between a spirit and a ghost?") I don't know the blessing, but it doesn't matter. I can't recognize the cemetery or my family's land.

'áádóó bik'įį', after that.

'áádoolzįįł, I shall discontinue it.

'aahasti', care, respect; care or respect toward a fragile object; fragility.[16]

'ąąh' azlá, pawn.

'ąąh 'dahaz'á, illness, sickness, an ailment.[17]

'ąąh dahoyooł'aałii, disease

'ąąh dah sitání, license plate.

'ąąh háá'á, debt.

'ąąh ha'ajeeh tó da'diisoołigíí, chicken pox.

'ąąh háát'i, fringes (saddle).

'ąąh naaznilę́ę̨, the pawns.

'ąąh nahóókadd, disappointment.

'ąąh ni'ít'aah, cast (plaster).

'aa hojoobá'í, poor.

'aahoolzhíísh, to be one's turn.

'ąąh sita', cervical.

'á'áhwiinít'į́, kindness.

'aa hwiinít'į, trial (at law), molestation.[18]

'aa hwiinít'į bá hooghan, courthouse.

'aahwiinít'įįgo, during the court session.

'aa hwiinít'įįhígíí, the court session that is to come.[19]

---

16 In "Confluence," MAL is defined as "a feeling of being watched from within."

17 September 19. I catch a cold from my students. Might be the flu. I tell Dibé Yázhí to stay away, but she says she won't get sick. We spend all day curled up on the couch watching *Shameless*. She rests her head on my shoulder, on my hip.

18 How are these words (kindness/molestation) that sound so similar, so different? My second dictionary is no help: it omits the second incident. My aunt tells my cousin that our grandmother molested her sons. My mother tells me other stories, similar but not the same. ("Why would they tell us that?") It's hard to believe, but it isn't. There will never be a trial. These are words better left unspoken, forgotten, erased.

19 September 16. Dibé Yázhí is told that if she doesn't appear for the court date, a warrant will be put out for her arrest. I agree to drive her back to the reservation on Monday night, after I am done teaching for the day. It is a six-hour drive, but I am almost happy to make it. I will be in Window Rock, with my family, on the two-year anniversary of my mother's death, not by plan but by circumstance.

'ą́ą́hyiłk'as, body chill.[20]

'áaji', up to that point; up to there; toward there; to that point and no farther.

'ááji', in that direction; on that side.

'aak'ee, fall, autumn.[21]

'aak'eedą́ą́', last fall, last autumn.

'aak'eego, in, or during the fall or autumn months.

'aak'eejí', near or close to the fall season.

'ąą kwáániił, it is expanding; it is getting bigger.[22]

'ááłdabidii'ní, we (pl.) mean by that.

'ááłdeiłní, they mean by that.

'aa'na' (ee'na'), yah, he crawled in (an enclosure, as a hole, house, etc.).

'aaníígóó, t'áá, the truth.[23]

'aaníinii, that which is true.

'aaníí, t'áá, it is true; truly; really; verily.[24]

20 I am sick with fever, alive with fever dreams. I dream of a two-story, sandstone motel, its three square walls opening onto the desert. A sun sets between two mountains, and heavy drapes are drawn across all the windows. My mother and my aunt and all my sisters are running in and out of the rooms, slamming doors, shouting at each other from the landings. I understand that each door is a choice, each room a potential future, and that my mother's and my aunt's and my sisters' doors are closed to me. Standing on the landing and looking into the sun, I notice a solitary woman's figure in the desert. She wears a loose blouse and a long skirt, cinched by an elaborate concho belt, and though I never met her, I know this woman is Pauline Tom, our gnomon, casting her long, indecipherable shadow on our lives.

21 August 2015. I am assigned two freshman composition classes my first year of graduate school. I am convinced that I have no idea what I am talking about; on the first day, I spend the entire hour sweating in front of my class. But afterward, two girls walk up to me and ask: What are your clans? Where is your family from? We are Navajo, too. We are all three nervous and unsure where the conversation should go, but I want to grab hold of them and root them next to me; graduation rates of native students are abysmally low.

22 September 22. After I drive Dibé Yázhí back home, she disappears in the middle of the night and leaves me and her mother a note: Went to Gallup. Need to get pads and face wash. Should be back soon. She leaves us a number, the wrong number. (My aunt says, "She prolly went to see *that guy*.")

23

24 My cousin-sister tells me she didn't see her boyfriend again. That she went over to a neighbor's and helped him set mouse traps in the middle of the night. He couldn't

'aaníí, t'áásh, is it so; is it true?[25]

'áánílígíí, that which is occurring; the happening; the event.[26]

'a'át'e', sin; injustice; meanness.

'áát'įįdę́ę, what he did; his aforementioned act.[27]

'aa yílyáii, donation.

'abąąh náát'i', border, strand (of the warp of a rug).[28]

'abaní, buckskin.

'abe', milk, teat, dug, pap.

'abe' 'astse', udder, mammary gland.

'abe'é, ch'il, milkweed.

'abéézh, there is boiling.

'abįda'diisdzil, they were forced to . . . .

'abid dijoolí, duodenum.

'ábi'diilyaa, he was made to be . . . . [29]

'ábidííniid, I said to him

'ábidiní, you say thus to him.

'ábidiní, ha'át'íí shą', what do you mean?[30]

do it himself, he kept catching his fingers. It is an elaborate, funny story to cover what feels like a lie. But she tells me she *would* tell me if she saw her boyfriend again.

25 The answer is, in many ways, unknowable. For our mothers, the surest protection from the past was to spin truths and falsehoods into one story, one thread, impossible to distinguish in the weave.

26 I have been walking around the thing that happened, stepping around the truth, trying to protect Dibé Yázhí from myself.

27 September 8. Dibé Yázhí called me at 4:30 in the morning, and I answered. She found out her boyfriend was cheating. She told me she started the fight, but he hit her. He threw her down, or she fell. Her voice was thick with tears. I know this story. I know it. These are words better left unspoken; a story better lost to time. Still, I had no words to help her. I will come get you, I told her. I will bring you home with me.

28 A Navajo blanket is woven on a fixed loom and will never outgrow its frame. Do we finish the story our mothers began, or do we rip out the weaving and begin anew? It is not so easy to erase or forget the things that have come before us.

29 . . . the kind of man who hits women. He crawled inside his father's shadow and filled it out.

30 One of my Navajo students interviews her aunt, who teaches Navajo language classes, and she writes a paper about revitalizing Diné Bizaad. I ask her if she would put me in contact with her aunt to answer some of my own questions. Her aunt

'**abi'doogį́**, he was hauled away.[31]
'**abi'dool'a'**, he was sent; he was commanded to go.
'**ábi'dool'įįdii, t'áá 'aaníí bee**, that with which he was really harmed.[32]
'**abi'doolt'e'ígíí, yah**, the fact that he was imprisoned.
'**abi'doolt'e, yah**, he was jailed, confined (as within an enclosure),
    imprisoned.[33]
'**ábidoołdįįł**, it will annihilate them.[34] '**ábidoołdįįłgo**, since it will
    annihilate.
'**ábidoo'niidę́ę**, what he was told; what he had been told.
'**ábiilaa**, it made him.
'**ábíłní**, he says to him.
'**abíní**, morning.[35]
'**abínídóó**, from the morning on . . . .
'**abnígo**, in the morning.
'**ábi'niidįįd**, it started to dwindle; it began to run out.
'**ábísdįįdii**, that which caused them to disappear, or become extinct.

agrees to email me her responses, but I am so lost, I don't know the right questions
to ask. I write a rambling email about adjectives and verbs and the state of being,
and she never responds.

31 When I was little, my mother called the cops on my father, often. Always after they
had both been drinking. I remember standing in the street with our neighbors and
watching the cops chase my father down the road, shove him into a police car, and
haul him away.

32 What are the roots of domestic violence on the reservation? Poverty. Untreated
mental illness. Self-medication through alcohol. Cycles of abuse: fathers beating
mothers beating sons beating their lovers and future mothers.

33 It wasn't his first time there, and he wasn't held long. He went home to his mother.

34 Rates of domestic violence and sexual assault are higher among Native Americans
than any other ethnicity in the United States. A study by the Centers for Disease
Control and Prevention from 2008 reported that almost 40 percent of Native
American women identified as victims of domestic violence during their lifetimes.
These are conservative figures; many assaults go unreported.

35 September 13. In my aunt's house, I wake before everyone and slip out of bed and
out the door with my cousin-brother's military binoculars. My aunt's dog, Toro,
follows me down the twisting dirt road and into the flowering sagebrush hills. Toro
follows his nose off the path, under bushes, over piles of gravel and rock. He misses
a pair of cottontails, who bolt out from under my feet as I cross the same ground
minutes later. They reach the safety of a hidden burrow before he turns around. The
cedar trees are full of birds.

'ábizhdííniid, he said to him.

'abízhí, paternal uncle or aunt.

'ábizh'niilaa, he started to make it.

'ach'ą́, hunger for meat.

'ách'ą́ą́h, in front of.[36]

'ach'ą́ą́h na'adá, protection.

'ách'ą́ą́h neilyéii, that which he protects himself by.

'achą́ą́ hwíídéeni, addiction.

'ach'é'é, daughter, niece (daughter of one's sister) (female speaking).[37]

'ach'é'édą́ą́', one's yard, or dooryard.[38]

'acheii (achaii), maternal grandfather.[39]

'achí, the act of giving birth.

'ách'į', toward oneself.

'áchįįh, nose, snout.[40]

'áchįįshtah, nostril, sinus.

36 September 22. My aunt and her neighbors clear the summer weeds out of the front yard and sweep them into piles. Toro has made a small rabbit's nest of them; he lies in a tight little ball. I call his name, and he lifts his head, fixes me with red, watery eyes, but he does not move.

37 After my mother dies, my aunt tells me that I am her daughter now—that she is my "little mother." This is how she introduces me to everyone: This is my niece! She's a teacher at the University of Arizona! This is how everyone responds: Hello, niece.

38 My maternal great-grandmother froze to death, and my aunt is shocked that I did not know. I don't understand because freezing to death in the desert, in the sun, surrounded by yellow sagebrush flowers, doesn't make sense to me. My aunt tells me Pauline Tom fell while checking on a noise outside, and she broke her hip in the fall. My aunt curls her hands on her skinny little wrists, mimes our grandmother, crawling in the dirt. She could not crawl far enough. My grandmother froze to death in the winter, in the deep dark of the night, in her own backyard.

39 I met my maternal grandfather once, when I was very young. He was a Navajo police officer. My aunt talked too soon about taking him off life support, then she and my mother stopped talking for years.

40 September 22. I call Toro's name again. On quivering legs, he hobbles over to me, then leans his whole weight against my body. "Toro," I whisper, tracing the black line between his eyes and smoothing my hands over his head and down his sides. I rub his soft ears, over and over. "It's so hard, I know. It's so hard." I think of the stories Dibé Yázhí told me. All the times he has been hit, flipped over the hoods of cars. Gotten up, shaken it off. Has he been hit again? My aunt won't take him to the vet. He's a Rez dog, now.

'áchį́įshtah dóó 'adáyi hashch'íí', catarrh.

'ach'į nahwii'ná, to have trouble; to have difficulty; to suffer.[41]

'ach'į na'ílyé, payment; to receive pension.

'ach'į niná'ílyá, repayment.

'acho', genitalia (male).[42]

'achó, maternal great-grandfather.[43]

'acho' biyę́ę́zhii, testicle.

'acho' bizis, prepuce.

'ach'ooní, comrade, partner.

'ada', nephew (son of one's sister) (male speaking).

'ádá, for self (myself, yourself, etc.).

'ádaa, to, about-self, concerning, to one-self. **'ádaa 'áhojilyą́**, he takes care of himself; he is on the alert.[44]

'adaa', lip.

'adą́ą́dą́ą́, yesterday.

'ádaadahalni'go, when they tell about themselves.[45]

'ádaadįįh, they are disappearing, about to disappear.

'ádaadin, they are none of them; they are non-existent, they are absent.[46]

41 My mother was homeless the six months leading up to her death, and she never called to ask me for help.

42 My other dictionary, Young and Morgan's, tells me **'achó** means maternal great-grand*mother* and that **'acho'** is not gendered. I am too embarrassed to ask for clarification, too scared my voice will betray me on the rising O.

43 In "Confluence," the taste of a maternal grandfather is CA PATA VATUZ.

44 My father would never admit his own violence, though I remembered it like a mirage in the desert—the images came back to me in shimmers, a disturbing gloss over the horizon.

45 When my mother dies, I am the one who must go through her things: her diaries, her letters, her photographs. She says things in writing she would never say to me herself, and I feel some validation of my own memory, my understanding. I let my cousin read some of her entries: There is truth in their stories, truth in our memories, if only we could let ourselves believe them.

46 Dr. William Morgan Sr., the linguist and translator for both Navajo dictionaries, passed away in 2001. He was eighty-five years old, nearly twice the age of my mother when she died. He received an honorary doctorate from the University of New Mexico and taught at Cornell, the University of New Mexico, and the Navajo Community College. According to his obituary, he left behind nineteen grandchildren and nineteen great-grandchildren. And though he is gone, he left a cultural

'ádaadinídíí, the ones that are gone; absentees; decedents.[47]

'ádaadzaa, they did.[48] **'ádaadzaa yę́ę́gi 'át'éego**, like they did.[49]

'ádaadzaaígi 'át'éego, like they did.[50]

'ádą̄ą̄h, upon oneself. **'ádą̄ą̄h áahast'ą́**, he committed a crime; made a serious mistake. **'ádą̄ą̄h dahosíst'ą́**, I committed a crime.[51]

legacy that will survive him and his children's children's children, perhaps.

47 I am unsure how many grandchildren and great-grandchildren survived Pauline Tom; there are too many blank spaces on the family tree my mother left behind. Many of my questions have no answers; the ones who could answer them are gone.

48 The court date is canceled. I find out after I leave that Dibé Yázhí is back with her boyfriend.

49 My mother would leave the men who hit her, but she would always take them back.

50 I should know better, but I don't. I hook up with men from the internet and drive long distances to meet them in hotel rooms. I let them tie me up, bruise my skin with ropes and clamps and leather, tear me up and make me bleed. I tell myself that it's okay because I let them—that I am the one with the power. I cannot tell if it is a lie, or if there is truth there, too.

51 I should not have taken her home. I should have spoken the words I meant to say. That we are worthy. That there is another path. That we can weave a rug of our own design. I started to look for those words but did not find them; I found only the same ghosts haunting the page.

War Baby

Jenny Boully

I myself was a war baby; so it would seem that I should be inden-
tured to this machinery, but I had already refused during first
period history to say the pledge of allegiance. My teacher scolded
me and said that we should, all of us, be willing to *die* for this
country, that his brother *died* for this country. Climbing milkweed was
overtaking the sky, and I walked home through alleyways, ditches, a
cut in chain link. I called a suicide hotline that night: I did not want to
allege myself to *anything*, not even *life*. To grow cruel and dark, a feral
underling: that was my adolescent calling. The walls of my room, covered with punk rock posters and concert flyers and antiwar slogans were
growing with it. The time came for loneliness; from the record shop by
the college campus downtown, I took the flyer but could not attend the
antiwar rally, which pledged that there should not be any blood for oil.
My best friend and her best friend deserted me. Somehow, I arranged
a date for myself with the college radio DJ and he let me drink beer
with him and his friends in the new club that opened, but then I saw

my old best friend there and she scratched at me and told the bouncer that I was drinking. I kept saying I was with the DJ and they let me go. Small complication: I was only fourteen. College DJ thought I was seventeen. I let the world go on while I wrote it all down in my diary. Using the address in Ann Landers, I sent the letter; she and her sister were always urging us to write and send care to the soldiers out there who were giving their blood for oil. The camouflage now was different from my daddy's. The new camouflage was made for this war in a desert, not the rain forests of Asia; still, it was made for a world where everything looked so similar to everything else that you couldn't see what might be happening right in front of you and so the camouflage made extra sure. It was the loneliness that had set in. I sent the letter with my fourteen-year-old self, her words and her picture, a picture that showed a girl wearing a tight black mini skirt, thigh-high stockings, lace-up boots up to her knees. A man from that war wrote back. He said a buddy of his had picked up my letter, saw my picture, and passed it on to him, saying I might be the one. I wrote back immediately; I needed love; all I had was my diary. There were rockets in the sky. Teachers at school were shocked: "You could see it on TV!" But I was not shocked or even surprised. Those flickers of light did nothing to unnerve me even though I kind of had a man there in that land of sand who might or might not have been close enough to see those rockets firsthand. They illuminated green on the screen, but I was not moved; after all, I had, always, seen everything on TV. It was, I thought, a beautiful thing, my reply in its pink envelope and flowery stationery, but I had included another complicated thing: I told the man that I was merely fourteen and sent a photo of me in fishnet stockings. He never wrote back. I did not yet know that love had its limits within its seemingly empty dimensions. I did not know that sometimes, for whatever reason, people lose interest. A year later, my mother came back to me, and, for her, I let my hair grow out as it should be, put away the clothes that got me in trouble. I got perfect As in school and began building difficult puzzles. The ones with 1,000 or more pieces were the ones that, being so impossible to complete with so much sky and forests of greens, kept me hidden at home, made it impossible for the boys to find me.

The Dry Season: Spring 2016

Melissa Febos

A t forty, while her interest in passionate friendship grew increasingly compelling, Virginia Woolf wrote to a friend that *"sexual* relations bore me more than they used: am I a prude? am I feminine? Anyhow for two years past, I have been a spectator of I daresay a dozen affairs of the heart—violent and crucial; and come to the conclusion that love is a disease; a frenzy; an epidemic; oh but how dull, how monotonous, and reducing its young men and women to what abysses of mediocrity!"[1]

I have been reading about Woolf because I am intrigued by the rumors of her celibate marriage.[2] Nearing the cusp of forty, after twenty years of consecutive intimate relationships, I have decided to spend three months celibate.[3]

+

1 Hermione Lee, *Virginia Woolf* (Vintage, 1997).
2 Her diaries and biography are also unparalleled tomes of juicy historical literary gossip.
3 It will become a celibate year, but thankfully I don't know that yet, nor that it will be the happiest year of my life.

At the end of May, I drive up to the Hudson Valley to stay with a friend I haven't seen for almost a year, not since I ended the two-year relationship that overtook my life and expedited my readiness for this celibate endeavor. That experience was less like sinking into an abyss of mediocrity (though it may also have been that, in effect) than being sucked into a maelström.

Edgar Allan Poe's 1841 short story, "A Descent into the Maelström," is a story within a story, told by a tour guide at a Norwegian mountain peak. On a fishing trip with his brothers, the narrator explains, his boat was swept by a hurricane into a voracious whirlpool. One of his brothers was swept to sea and drowned and the other went mad at the sight of it.

The guide witnessed the vortex first as an abominable monster, then as a sublime creation. Observing the movement of the maelström's pull on different objects, he clung to a barrel and eventually was rescued. He explains to his audience that while he looks aged, with white hair and a haggard face, he is not old but was instantly transformed by the ordeal.

It was this story that introduced the word *maelström* into the English language. Poe based his maelström on the Moskstraumen, a famous system of whirlpools in the Lofoton archipelago, off the coast of Norway, exceptional for its occurrence in the open sea—most whirlpools occur in more constrained waterways.[4]

I was shocked to find myself captive in such a maelström at thirty-two years old and ten years sober; it would have made more sense had it occurred during the more dire straits of my twenties. But like the

---

4 The Moskstraumen also appears in Jules Verne's *Twenty Thousand Leagues Under the Sea*, and is mentioned by Melville's Captain Ahab in *Moby-Dick*.

Mosckstraumen, whose odd location is due to a configuration of tides, local winds, and underwater topographies, my maelström was presaged by the invisible topographies of my early life and precipitated by a series of local events that rendered me vulnerable to a powerful and seemingly unlikely phenomenon.

It is easy to imagine that relationship as an abominable monster—not my lover, nor exactly myself, but the centripetal force activated by our merging. There was a third thing, a thing that had not enacted so fiercely in me before or after her. If the mathematical sublime, as Kant articulated it, can be evidenced by finding something fearsome without being afraid of it, then I did not see my maelström as a sublime creation. I was terrified by it, by myself at every moment of it.[5]

Now, at some years' distance, I can see with a more passive astonishment the magnitude of that power, the psychic physics that sprung a tornado in me. I know that potential still resides, and I revere it, as some people do their gods or volcanoes, in hope that it won't enact its power against me again.

+

As I drive to visit my friend whom I have not seen since the maelström, I feel like that guide at the summit—my hair gone white, my nerves ruined, but restored insofar as it is possible. I have not only strayed from the self I was before, but been changed. One doesn't *restore* a house that

5 Immanuel Kant et al., *The Critique of Judgement* (Clarendon, 1982).

has been demolished or burned to its foundation; one rebuilds. I feel sheepish, chastened by the memory of my behavior when I was beside myself.

All of this to say: A friend who has seen you in the throes of an abusive relationship is similar to those friends who saw you at your addicted bottom. Both have seen you out of control, in one kind of blackout or another—powerless. They have seen you in ways that you could not see yourself. This dynamic is the foundation of so much humiliation and intimacy. The same principle of vulnerability renders the back of the neck and knee erotic. Childhood and very old age aside, it is possible for many to get through most of life avoiding this.

I heard someone say once in a recovery meeting that an alcoholic would rather die than be embarrassed. I don't think it's only alcoholics, though we do have more to be embarrassed about.

I am shy to see my friend, but happy to greet her familiar impish face. I am grateful for her gentleness when we revisit the past. When I think of my last visit to her rambling, toy-strewn upstate house, it is like remembering a bad dream or scary movie: a madwoman careening around the curves of the Taconic Parkway, eyes flashing but empty like those of someone possessed by a demon.

Sometimes, when I think of it, I picture the poster of Hitchcock's 1958 noir film, *Vertigo*. *Vertigo* is full of spirals. The opening credits feature an animated spiral revolving in neon colors, and a close-up of a dictionary entry for the word *vertigo* that reads: ". . . figuratively, a state in which all things seem to be engulfed in a whirlpool of terror." The characters of the film are captive in a whirl of distorted reality whose principal activator is love. There is a murder plot, but at its core, *Vertigo* is a story of romantic obsession and its consequences, the terrors that become possible in that altered psychic landscape.

My past self is a stranger, an imposter who inhabited my life for two years. The mental pain was acute and relentless, and like all sufferers of acute pain I was only half awake to any other experience, perhaps less. We are taught that obsession is romantic, but it is not. It is hell.

+

Philip Glass was commissioned to write a score for the Australian Dance Theater's adaptation of Poe's short story, which was performed at the 1986 Adelaide Festival of Arts. The Philip Glass Ensemble plays the score, which is anxiety and terror, made musical, while two dancers cling to a mast in the center of the stage. A female dancer whirls vigorously around them, her body a frothing wave, soon joined by others. It is a faithful representation of the story, and of my experience in the maelström: relentless, thrilling, and exhausting. Like the *Vertigo* trailer promises, it is "a story that gives new meaning to the word suspense."

+

When I tell my friend about my celibacy, she tells me that she, too, has been in nonstop relationships since her teens. She, too, has often felt in some deep part of herself that she needed a break. I tell her about my morning sheet angels, and how it has come to seem like so many people are drunk driving through their lives, getting high off of other people. I am happier than I have been in years, I tell her. I am happier, perhaps, than I have ever been. Being alone is a kind of ecstasy, I explain. Then I feel a little awkward, because she is married with a child and ostensibly will never get a break, will never know the pleasure of aloneness. It seems rude that I have brought this to our attention, as if I am a rich friend flaunting my wealth to a poorer friend.

+

The psychotherapist has written a very wise book with a very bad title. A mutual friend recommended I read it and was correct in her prediction that I would find it helpful. After I return to the city, we meet for lunch at Coffee Shop in Union Square. When I arrive, she has already secured a booth. She is tiny, dressed in a drapey linen outfit and artistic jewelry. She epitomizes a type of therapist that I like (small, Jewish, bossy) and I like her immediately, though she says many things with which I disagree.

You define yourself too much as an addict, she tells me. What is an addict but someone who is dealing with some unresolved element?

What are any of us but that? I counter.

I think your sexual hiatus is brilliant, she says. And that without it you'll keep doing the exact same thing.

I've begun to wonder if three months is long enough, I confide.

She laughs. Are you kidding me? Try starting with six months. She sets down her fork for emphasis. It has to be hard, she says. If it's not hard, you're not doing it.

I don't agree, but I like her certainty.

You know Ulysses? she asks.

Of course, I say.

You have to lash yourself to the mast. It has to be that hard.

I laugh at this. She is so dramatic!

You know what I think is going happen? she says. I think you're going to get depressed. Really depressed. Possibly suicidal. She shrugs. Maybe not, but don't be surprised. There's something you must be hiding from. You have to give yourself space to do that. Without it you'll still be in prison. You have to let yourself wake up. It can't be a stunt.

+

Waking alone is so far one of the principal pleasures of celibacy. I stretch my limbs out until I am eagle spread, then make sheet angels on the white cotton. There is no one to text who will be mad that I haven't responded. Sometimes I ignore my phone for hours after waking.

Now that it is mine alone, I am becoming something of a bed fetishist. I have replaced the pillows and sheets, and ordered a new mattress. It arrives compressed in a box and when freed, swells like a sponge until it covers the floor. It is already hot outside so I take a shower and then lie on the new bed and masturbate in front of the air conditioner.[6]

---

6 My abstinence doesn't preclude masturbation; it has never been a compulsive practice. It is my relationships with people that are the issue, the thing from which a respite will do me good.

+

I have increasingly stopped eating meal-appropriate foods at the appropriate mealtime. Instead, when I get hungry I eat a plate of pickles and cheese, dried fruit and nuts, a sliced apple maybe, at any time of day or night. In the middle of the night, I wander into the kitchen and eat pickles straight out of the jar by the light of the open refrigerator, though this practice predates my celibacy.

Pythagoras is better known for his eponymous theorem (whose authorship is debated) but he also founded a cultish school whose members—both male and female—were sworn among other things to secrecy, vegetarianism, and celibacy, but only in the hot "dry" seasons of summer and fall. Winter, apparently, was safer for sex in its wetness. Conversely, early ascetics and doctors often believed that drying out the body was necessary for celibacy. Food that they deemed drying included many legumes,[7] vinegars, salted olives, and dried fruit. None of this informs my own eating decisions, but as a secretive, celibate vegetarian with a taste for vinegars and dried fruit, the parallels do please me.

+

---

7 Pythagoras wouldn't eat legumes because he thought them the "first child of the earth." The fava bean in particular, he and his acolytes believed to be a supernatural symbol of death. According to Pliny, he even believed them capable of carrying the souls of the dead (a fact mocked by Horace, who called fava beans "Pythagoras' children," and other Greeks, who ate them frequently). Though he became something of a laughingstock for his vegetarian diet (known more as a Pythagorean diet then, and in some places until the nineteenth century), and his related belief in metempsychosis (the theory of transmigration of souls), he inspired the likes of Seneca, Ovid, and Plutarch, the last of whom wrote quite a bit about his reasons for not eating meat.

After the maelström, I had a series of short-lived affairs. The most surprising of these was a tryst with a twenty-five-year-old. I had never dated anyone younger than me, and she was a decade my junior. When I confessed this to my sponsor, she shrugged. We were both consenting adults, she pointed out, but still I knew it was proof that I was unhinged.

After the twenty-five-year-old, I dated an age-appropriate DJ for five months. When I began dating the DJ, I called the twenty-five-year-old to tell her it was definitively over, though I had been careful to warn her the whole time that it couldn't ever be serious. What twenty-five-year-old heeds a careful warning? *No!* she shouted into the phone, sounding more like a child than ever before. I felt embarrassed for us both: her for acting a child, me for dating her, though I was always careful not to call it that.

I met the DJ at the lesbian bar where she spun on Thursday nights. I was dancing a lot at the time. My friend May and I would go out at 11 p.m. and dance until 2 a.m. multiple nights per week. It was the longest I'd ever been single and I was manic with relief after the agony of the maelström. Though I felt hollowed out afterward, aged ten years in two, the summer that followed felt like an enchantment: the heat luscious, time gone soft and plastic, each morning marked by my aching feet, the pleasurable wince as I brewed coffee in the morning.

The DJ was beautiful, intelligent, and kind. She also smoked weed and cigarettes every day and drank not a small amount. She lived with a roommate and a gorgeous Persian cat who pissed on everything. When she arrived home in the early hours of morning, there was often a pile of cat shit waiting on her bedroom floor.

The first time I tried to break up with her, I couldn't bear how sad she looked. I backpedaled and said we should just spend less time together. A few weeks later, I said that we should spend even less time together. A few weeks later, I suggested that we open the relationship. When I finally broke up with her, she squinted at me.

You're terrible at this, huh? she said. Breaking up with people.

Yes, I said. It was actually one of my more successful tries.

+

In the past, I sometimes stayed in relationships for months and months after I knew I wanted to leave, until eventually I became attracted to someone else and kissed them. Of course, people in committed relationships are often attracted to other people; it doesn't necessarily mean that a breakup is imminent or necessary, or that kissing is, though in my case it usually was. I willed myself to stay, but after a certain amount of time my body would revolt. I never stayed past the first kiss—I don't have the constitution for a protracted affair[8]—but also rarely had the guts or gumption to break it off without the imperative of infidelity. This is not something I am proud of, though I do recognize that I have been conditioned by a history that stretches back centuries.

I was not bound to any lover by the thirteenth-century common law of "coverture," which persisted throughout the eighteenth and

---

8 Not exactly true. I actually think my default constitution is exactly oriented to be capable of protracted affairs—I am adept at compartmentalizing, have a compulsive nature and poor impulse control, and am powerfully swayed by the hormonal pull of attraction. I have, however, been sober for more than a decade and the work of that time has been that of cultivating a consciousness and a set of instincts counter to my given disposition.

nineteenth centuries, in which marriage essentially erased a woman's sole legal identity, so that her rights and property were *cover*ed by her husband's. Breaking up with lovers would not render me destitute nor a social exile, but it sometimes felt that way, as if the stakes were inexplicably high. I would grapple for a rational estimation of loss to explain my dread, but there was none.

But we laugh so often together! I might offer to my therapist or friends, hearing how impotent the explanation sounded. I have always laughed with my lovers; I am a person who likes to laugh. I didn't know how else to explain the terrible fear of leaving them. The specter of a commensurate loss must be somewhere, I reasoned. It was, but beyond the scope of my own life. It was less than a hundred years before my birth that women were allowed to remain legal entities after marriage and could avoid losing everything by breaking up.

Not to mention that sex beyond marriage guaranteed social ruination and divorce was all but unheard of until the mid-nineteenth century, and even then exceedingly difficult for a woman to justify. While a wife's adultery was adequate reason for a man to divorce her, she must prove bigamy, incest, cruelty, or desertion in addition to adultery.[9]

We have heard of all of this, seen the frothy period films that romanticize it and the tragedies inherent, but when I look at the earnest effort with which I have sought to justify my desire to end relationships of even just a few months, my belief that I needed justification far

---

9 A New Hampshire court denied a woman divorce in 1836, despite the fact that her husband had locked her in a cellar and beaten her with a horse whip while spewing insults, because she had a "high bold, masculine spirit" that had rendered her unwifely. The court decided that it was up to her to improve herself and thus her marriage.

beyond my own desire to leave, it is hard not to factor in the stakes of the past.

+

The DJ and I are on good terms and when I ask if I can buy her lunch in exchange for help assembling my new bedframe, she agrees. The bedframe is from IKEA and it is missing an important screw. The slat apparatus is confoundingly complex. We walk to three hardware stores in the gummy heat to find a replacement screw. It takes the whole afternoon with a break for pad thai, and afterward I pay for her cab to the lesbian bar. Alone again, I lie on my new bed, tacky with dried sweat, ecstatically alone. In the lesbian Olympic games, assembling IKEA furniture that is missing screws on a team with your ex would be an advanced category and we would have just earned a gold medal.

+

Perhaps even more compelling and difficult to prize out of one's consciousness is the narrative that accompanied the idea of marital love. Heralded by Jane Austen's novels published at the threshold of the Victorian period, wifedom and motherhood were considered in addition to the primary route to financial stability as that to personal fulfillment and self-actualization. The combination of these imperatives, while no longer concretely viable for many of us, persists in an insidious legacy that has affected even my queer relationships. Like Kelli María

Korducki: "I've long suspected that women subconsciously accept some version of the belief that we're supposed to want secure romantic relationships more than anything in the world."[10]

+

Let's say that there are three kinds of ecstasy, though of course, there are many more. Physical ecstasy, as in an orgasm. Mental ecstasy, as in the particular arrangement of brain chemicals (serotonin, dopamine, oxytocin, adrenaline) that produce a high. And spiritual ecstasy, which is primary the ecstasy of self-forgetting, a total engrossment and devotion to something other than the self. I would categorize the total self-forgetting that can sometimes result of both dancing and writing under spiritual ecstasy, as did Aristotle.

"Perfect joy excludes even the very feeling of joy," writes Simone Weil, "for in the soul filled by the object no corner is left for seeing 'I.'"[11]

+

The pleasure of watching television I would not categorize among the ecstasies, though it is a form of standing outside oneself, as the original *ekstasis* is defined. In the early weeks of my celibacy, I indulged in long hours of well-written British dramas and police procedurals. Now, I am struggling.

10 Kelli María Korducki, *Hard to Do: The Surprising, Feminist History of Breaking Up* (Coach House Books, 2018).
11 Simone Weil, *Gravity and Grace* (Routledge, 2002).

Have the stories available for our entertainment always centered the overwhelmingly heterosexual romances and tragedies of marriage and parenthood? Even when the outlier show that features a queer character as more than a gossipy sidekick or punchline manages to get produced, it is almost exclusively about the dating and sexual travails of that queer character, often in a mode dynamically indistinguishable from its heterosexual counterpart.

I scroll through the infinite offerings and watch trailer after trailer. It is difficult to find one show about a woman who doesn't have children or a partner and isn't trying to get either.

+

"As long as she thinks of a man," wrote Virginia Woolf, "nobody objects to a woman thinking." Woolf's father allowed more room for her thinking than many late nineteenth-century fathers, but seemingly just enough to realize how little she had, how constrained not only by her patriarchal society but also by the patriarchs of her particular life. He was seventy-two when he died (Virginia, twenty-two), and she imagined that if he had lived longer, "his life would have entirely ended mine . . . No writing, no books;—inconceivable." Still, his figure dominated her early works and journals, asserting itself at the center of her consciousness as he had her life when alive.

I am interested in the way that thinking of a man, or any person, can dictate not only the course of one's life but also that of one's art. Liberation of the mind can be essential to a liberation of art.

+

Yes, the stories of women have most often revolved around men, marriage, and motherhood. It just didn't bother me this much before. It didn't *bore* me this much before. I was able to enjoy a wide assortment of treacly dramas, manipulative thrillers, or sharp-witted and predictable comedies, the way I'm able to enjoy a delicious but unnourishing snack. In fact, with a similar voraciousness to that which consigns me to the occasional sickened hangover. There can be a pleasure, tinged with relief, in yielding to the entertainments I have been conditioned to absorb. Reinforcement is more comfortable than subversion. Now, I am increasingly unable to forget that what I am watching is reinforcing my own conditioning, further obscuring my actual interests and priorities. I can no longer enjoy what is making me sick.

When I was a dominatrix in my twenties, I used to enjoy indulging in celebrity tabloids. I'd always dismissed them with a sneer, but my colleagues would leave them discarded around our dressing room, like slippery portals into a world where the diets of strangers constituted headlines and only a tiny fraction of the female population seemed to age beyond thirty-five.

When I quit sex work, I couldn't stomach paying for these magazines, but still relished scavenging them among the free reading materials at the gym. I would climb the towering escalator to nowhere while flipping mindlessly through comparisons of emaciated starlets' abdomens. Who wore it better? Who had lost her man to a younger, more emaciated woman? Who had dared don a swimsuit after gaining five pounds?

When I think back on this it is like remembering drinking poison.

I have always thought that I simply trailed off reading these tabloids, or maybe aged out of them, but now I can see that I stopped reading them exactly when I stopped dating men.

+

Vera is a long-running British crime series adapted from crime novelist Ann Cleeves's books, starring Brenda Blethyn as DCI Vera Stanhope, a curmudgeonly detective in her sixties who dresses like Paddington Bear, lives a solitary lifestyle, and probably qualifies as a workaholic. She seems to have no sexual interest in anyone. Her passions are for solving murders and eating biscuits. She is fat, charismatic, brilliant, disheveled, sometimes aggressive with her colleagues, intolerant of the sentimental and bullshit equally, and likes to have a young male sergeant to boss around. She never expresses regret about not having children, in whom she is wholly uninterested. Now in its eleventh season, each episode draws upwards of eight million viewers in the U.K. Vera is beloved. She is one of the few examples I could find, almost all of which feature female detectives.

As she thinks about murder, nobody objects to a woman thinking.

+

When I was younger and eating disordered, I spent most of my waking time (and some of my sleep) thinking about food. Sometimes, I would imagine the time and energy I had spent thinking about food amassed, how enormous it would be. I could write a book with it, I'd think. Similarly, the many-years obsession with controlling the shape of my body. Also, heroin—procuring it, ingesting it, withdrawing from it.

I have probably spent more time thinking about lovers past present and future than any of those other obsessions. I could write several books with that cumulative energy (arguably, I have). I could have run for office. I could have gotten a PhD. I could have had an entire supplementary career. I could have become a real activist instead of just someone who writes about the things she'd like to change.

+

Everything you write is about love, a friend once said to me. It wasn't a compliment but a complaint. So what, I thought, though I was unsettled because I had not noticed this before she pointed it out.

+

Are you single? Diana texts me.

Yes, I say. Although I am celibate until at least mid-August.

I want to set you up with someone, she says.

In mid-August, I say. A few minutes later, the prospective date texts me. We flirt for a few exchanges and then I end it.

See you in August, I type.

Thanks for the endorphins, she replies. Afterward, my body is warm, as if someone has turned the dial up, flipped my switch. I think of how recognizable it now is in other people, that buzzy high. Now it is I who is sparking inside, the stranger a flint I've struck myself against. Not even a hard surface is required, it seems. My excitement curdles into a mucky feeling, as if I have cheated. Have I cheated? I'm the only one who can say.

It's always a question of how honest one wants to be with oneself. I mean, why bother with such a project if I'm not going to be whole-hearted about it? Still, half measures are worth something. I've committed greater cons on myself than fake celibacy.

+

Emma and I plan to meet at the afterparty of an awards show. She is the last person with whom I was involved, after the twenty-five-year-old, the DJ, and a short list of others that includes the last man I will ever have dated. When we met, Emma was married. Now, she is less married. We are trying to be friends and succeeding somewhat. The DJ is the DJ of the afterparty. When I arrive at the party, my partner in the maelström is there. I have not seen her since I ended the relationship. Surveying the room, my hands grow sweaty and I feel like crying or leaving but I don't cry and I don't leave. I dance. I dance until I don't care if any of my exes are watching, until my thighs sing with exhaustion, until I am as happy as sex has ever made me.

While we wait at the bar for a cup of water, Emma looks around.

Maybe you should stop shitting where you eat, she says.

I have, I say. It just hasn't been very long.

188

+

Sometimes, it is hard to tell what is a condition of being a queer woman dating in New York City and what is a condition of being me.

+

At the end of the night, the DJ and I share a cab back to our neighborhood. She asks for a kiss before exiting the cab.

No, I say. The no rings like a gong through my body until I fall asleep.

I have said yes so many times to appease other people. That is, to avoid the discomfort of displeasing other people. A way to write one of the equations in the problem of my celibacy would be to say that the discomfort of paying my body for that passage grew greater than the discomfort of displeasing others.

"I'd had it with handing myself over," as Sophie Fontanel writes.[12] While I lie in bed, listening to the reverberation of that no, the difference is clear. The discomfort of others' displeasure is fleeting. It isn't mine. They take it with them when they go. The discomfort of betraying my body's wishes, of betraying myself to appease my aversion to others' displeasure—that lingers. I am thick with it.

What body could trust the person who did that to her? What person could trust her body?

12 Sophie Fontanel, *The Art of Sleeping Alone: Why One French Woman Suddenly Gave Up Sex* (Scribner, 2017).

Watercourses

Wendy S. Walters

Before I saw the pictures of the cars submerged in water at a dip in the interstate or the trucks pumping water out of the warehouse basements near the river, my mother described how low the water table had been all year, how the whole region had been on the verge of a drought. She said the rain had been needed though no one expected so much of it to fall all at once. In the morning my sister and I went for a walk by the river. I told her she was not drinking enough water. I said I wanted her to take better care of her own health—to not just focus on everyone else in her family. We were surprised to see the street strewn with wood chips and the flood still receding. That day it was still easy to pretend that we did not understand the magnitude of the change, how soon it would happen again, how far beyond the riverfront the water had traveled inland without regard for the lines drawn on the map, the boundaries of municipality. I lectured my sister, but my own health had been suffering for nearly three years. I sought a diagnosis, occasionally giving up on feeling better between appointments with specialists. My symptoms had been complicated, but they were also consistent. I also had the sense that my doctors were not listening to me, were not recognizing my pain as something that could be addressed through efforts beyond my own. This is not the point of the story, but I need to be clear I was talking to them about agony, not discomfort.

By the next day, most of the streets by the riverfront had been swept clean and the remaining evidence of the flood, at least on the street level, was hard to see. But I heard reports on the local news about wet basements, concerns about mold growing deep in the walls. It was so bad that the president promised to come and survey the damage. This was also an opportunity for him to connect with some of the people who did not vote for him, who might vote for him the next time. In the coming weeks, the Supreme Court would allow one more state to continue with their plans to restrict access to voting, and I felt despair about these limits to citizenship. What frustrated me in the moment was my inability to imagine the future, a skill I had always relied on in my times of deep concern or despair. I never expected my vision of the future to be predictive or correct, but I did believe the space of imagination could help me to endure the harsh facts of the moment. Dan and I went for a walk down by the river, and it was crowded with people. There were several new babies who could barely hold their heads up. A dragonfly landed on my shirt and rested there for nearly a quarter of a mile. In the evening, my sister sent me a picture from the lake. In the light of a car's headlights, there were thousands of mayflies. They don't have mouths because they don't eat. Most will not live more than a day. The female ones will die within five hours.

I wrote to apologize to a student for my delayed response to their message and to confess that I was dealing with a family emergency. What I didn't say was that the emergency was mine, that I had spent the night in the emergency room for a chronic condition I don't regularly discuss. I was suffering from a problem of volume, the anguish of swelling and receding. In the hospital, I distracted myself by listening to other people's pain, most of which was more acute than mine. One man had cracked his skull open in a fall and needed surgery. His brain was *ok*, the doctor assured him. A young couple suspected they had contracted Covid, though despite their discomfort they remained uninterested in the vaccine. In the late hours, another man pleaded in hunger for fish sticks. I appreciated the specificity of his desire. After I woke the next day, I felt guilty because I knew I would not be able to get much done. I am always working, and I am always behind. Another student wrote with a minor request, and again I felt compelled to answer right away. But I still felt weak and could barely stand. I needed to sleep, but I did not try to make myself comfortable. The rain stopped, and the sun came out, but I could still smell a restlessness in the air. Elsewhere there has been catastrophic heat all summer, sparking fires and many deaths, especially in northern cities where people do not yet know how to live with it.

A few days later while working at the kitchen table, a small brown rabbit came all the way up to the front door before I saw it. When it noticed me, it was neither afraid nor distracted from its own curiosity. Dan watched a pheasant strutting up the drive, but when we got up to get a closer look at it, it ran down the road with the accuracy of an arrow. The fact is that I was still wobbly, not just due to the facts of my body but also due to the vagaries of my intentions, which were vexed thanks to my sense of foreboding about the future. The next few days were hot and humid, but then once again we expected several days of thunderstorms. Six in a row as far as the meteorologist's predictions assessed. There was water in the air—humidity—but also a heaviness of understanding. I mean that the water was saying something I didn't understand. I worried I would never understand. I do know that all water is related to itself, no matter what lines of belonging we draw for it on the map. I also know that everywhere people live there are waterways buried, rivers that have been biding time to resurfacing, watercourses long paved over for the sake of industry and convenience. Where these undercurrents flow is often only revealed after a flood. Once it recedes, it can seem as though it will be gone forever. I knew better, but I still had to remind myself to not forget. Maybe it was the water in the air that made me feel dumb, as logic and anxiety swam around my consciousness.

When I went to get my prescription filled, I realized the ER doctor had incompletely notated my diagnosis, which I explained to her at the intake with great care, given that the treatment I was under was for a chronic condition. She listed only one of my symptoms, the easiest one to spell, even though I showed her test results from my most recent diagnosis. I explained my pending surgery, but she wrote nothing about it down. Then she authorized bloodwork I did not want done, tests I did not consent to. I thought about her dumb hands searching inside of me for the relief of recognition in my parts, all accounted for. Days later I was still ashamed to have met her with compassion and understanding for the stress she must have felt that night. I felt disappointed in myself for not having responded to her coldly or with disdain. I became a reservoir of anger that night, possibly misdirected, but it was raining again. The two mosquito bites on my arm were inflamed. I realized, not for the first time, that my favorite color is the blue gray of clouds passing by after an early evening storm.

I complained to Dan about all I needed to get done before the summer's end, all the necessary steps each task required, and he responded that there were too many things. He said I was flooding him. It was raining again. The street parallel to ours was already full of water. So was the one after that. On the local news, there was talk of the cars submerged on the interstate once again. There was even a clip of a man driving his van into a large puddle then abandoning it once he realized he could not make it through. He laughed when the newscaster reached him to ask, "What were you thinking?" The man said, "I thought I could make it," which is probably what we will all think at some point soon. When the rain began the next day or the day after that, to be honest I was starting to lose track at this point, I saw the brown rabbit calmy resting under a broad leaf in the middle of the empty lot next door. I remembered rabbit fur is coated in lanolin, which keeps them from truly feeling wet unlike its predators who may have sought shelter beneath the porches or in the drainpipes. Why hide from the weather with those who might do you in if you are lucky enough to be unbothered by the rain?

My doctor back home responded to my note about my night in the

ER by saying it was time to call the surgeon. The surgeon said there was no more time to postpone treatment, so I booked my procedure for the following Monday. The risk was not that I would bleed to death, necessarily, but that I might make other parts of my body sick if I waited much longer to address the problems I already had. The procedure was scheduled for an outpatient facility. All went very well, the surgeon assured me. He said the intensity of the pain I felt meant I was getting better. But when it was time for me to get up and go home, I could not do it. The rest of the floor was already dark and vacant. I struggled to stand then doubled over. I asked for a wheelchair but couldn't put myself in it. I started to spit up water. After that, I felt light enough for a moment to throw myself into the chair, my legs shaking as they wheeled me to the car. I held a bucket on my lap, which I hoped not to need. I didn't open my eyes. I suspected if I didn't look where I was heading, I wouldn't get sick. But every time I tried to peer out of the darkness, even just a little, I felt water rising at the back of my throat. I hoped I wouldn't be overcome when I opened the car door at the steps of my building, but it came rushing out of me again.

In the shelter of my own room, my courage evaporated, and I suffered openly, properly. I felt my pain more intensely than all other commitments and let myself wade through the magnitude of it all night. I had become so used to being in pain that I rarely thought about what it would be like if it were not there, except for those times I read something exploring what it is to live with "chronic pain." I have wondered: *what must it feel like to be in pain all the time?* while forgetting about my own. I am not at the phase of life where I can acknowledge pain socially; it would be just one more thing that is my fault. People would ask, *do you have a diagnosis?* Which sounds to me like, *how is this your fault?* But I also know that no diagnosis could solve the way one's own pain does not measure up to the expectation of others. How horrible it would be to discover that what I knew intimately of pain was not actually pain at all but rather, practically not a bother to those who have made better choices than I have, those more practiced in endurance. Maybe what I have mistaken for pain is just my life.

When pain does not deliver permanent change, such as disability or death, it also appears to change nothing in the story. This is also the truth of a flood. For my part, I was not interested in telling a story about my pain or anyone else's, unless it also takes time to account for how that pain has made a world. A few weeks ago, my sister drove over to the apartment, and we sat outside on the front lawn. First thing she wanted to talk about was money. This was not something that either of us grew up discussing, but now that we have children, we both think about money all the time. To simplify our different perspectives on the subject, one could say that I think about money as space, and she thinks about it as time. We both think about money as a way to mitigate pain, but that is the part of the conversation we did not have because we do not talk that way with each other. Like all the women we know who talk about money, we were thinking about death, too. Our yearnings that day seemed more aligned than when we were younger and lived in discordant tempos. We confessed that we wanted to walk more, to spend more time with our families, and to work on our own terms.

My mother told me the story of someone she knew who, after the first flood several weeks ago, had her basement drained then replaced all the appliances, including the furnace and hot water heater. As soon as the workmen finished installing the new washer and dryer, she saw water running down the basement steps once again. My mother told me this as we walked across a bridge over the interstate. Its grassy slopes were untended, overrun with weeds and wildflowers that seem to be appreciated by the Monarch butterflies, who stop near the river as they migrate to Mexico at the end of summer. The difference between a butterfly and moth is how they hold their wings. A butterfly holds its wings erect, up over its back, while a moth holds its wings as if covering itself, signaling a cautiousness that misrepresents the magnitude of its potential flight.

The next night the rain came down in sheets again, but the city did not flood. In the morning I heard there were also tornados this time, though they had touched down several miles north. I sat on my mother's couch and watched the evening's news. The weekend weatherman seemed delighted as he gave his forecast for the next week, which would present with a mix of clouds and rain. He had that same look in his eye when he talked about storms now as he did back when we briefly dated in college. Decades later, he had become exactly the meteorologist he had always wanted to be with more and more unusual weather on the horizon every passing year. How did he know? I am in the part of my life when past feels both far away and near. I am not angry at time, though I don't understand its capacity to collapse my realizations from different times into simultaneous events. By this point my pain was starting to feel less severe, and I felt a little melancholy as it started to slip away, as I thought I might lose some of myself along with my understanding of it. I wondered who I might become without it to lodge me in a predictable state of distress. *There will be more pain*, I thought, to comfort myself as I looked out to the darkening street. A small black kitten lingered on the sidewalk. The air smelled like ragweed and optimism. In the morning my sister told me about swelling in her legs, and I encouraged her to get herself checked out by a doctor, soon. I asked if she was drinking enough water.

We drove around the flooded streets performing surprise at how deep the water was each time. We pretended to be shocked when someone told us about a flood in their home. A worry grew between all of us that was deeper than regret. It might have been rage. And what about the rabbits? I stopped seeing them after the tornados. Perhaps they moved along to some other field, or maybe they drowned. I know nothing. My sister looked more tired than she did at the start of the summer, or maybe it was me who looked so weary. We put on our sneakers and went down to the river. My knees were swollen or was it her ankles? A man sped past us on a bicycle, playing a song on his speaker. What was that song? I looked at the river, and it flickered back at me infuriatingly blue. My sister and I talked about the pain in her legs, in my legs, but I was hesitant to confess to her what I know. I told her she needs to take care of herself because everyone is counting on her. As soon as I said that I saw the weight of my request on her face. One more thing. Then it went away as if she had forgotten what I said entirely. She asked me questions about my plans for the autumn, my plans to come back home next summer. She was very chipper. It was not possible for me to think that far ahead, and I regretted not being able to make a promise. Then I let go of that feeling, and we kept walking.

Acknowledgments

Without the support of many wonderful people and publications, this book would not have been possible.

Thank you to the New Books Network's "New Books in Literature" channel (newbooksnetwork.com) and Ander Monson and Will Slattery at Essay Daily (essaydaily.org) for providing the space for our initial conversations about the lyric essay.

We want to thank the original three members of our "Lyric Essay as Resistance" panel at the Association of Writers and Writing Programs Conference in 2020: Lyzette Wanzer, Jenny Boully, and Krys Malcolm Belc for thoughtfully engaging this conversation about the lyric essay and extending our thinking in unexpected ways, and to all twenty of our amazing contributors, whose work continues to inspire us.

Thank you to Stephanie Williams for her faith in the project from its inception. Thanks, too, to our wonderful acquisitions editors, Annie Martin and Marie Sweetman, for their support and guidance, as well as the dedicated team at WSUP who worked to bring this book into the world.

Big thanks to Elena Passarello and Marjorie Sandor at Oregon State University for their early support of our anthology dreams.

Thank you to Kristina Tate, Kara Williams, and Laura Laing for their friendship, writerly camaraderie, and hosting us at Creekside, where we developed parts of this project.

Finally, thanks to our families: Jason and Dowker, Adam and Dot, for your love and support.

With thanks to the original venues of publication in which these works appeared:

"Dreaming of Ramadi in Detroit." Copyright © 2017 by Aisha Sabatini Sloan, from *Dreaming of Ramadi in Detroit*. Reprinted by permission of 1913 Press.

"Architectural Survey Form: 902 Sunset Strip." Copyright © 2019 by Camellia-Berry Grass, from *Hall of Waters*. Reprinted by permission of Camellia-Berry Grass.

"The Story You Never Tell." Copyright © 2019 by Chelsea Biondolillo, from *The Skinned Bird*. Reprinted by permission of KERNPUNKT Press.

"A Meditation on Grief: The Things We Carry, the Things We Remember." Copyright © 2021 by Crystal Wilkinson, from *Perfect Black*. Reprinted by permission of University Press of Kentucky.

"The Little Girl, Her Drunk Bastard Parents, and the Hummingbird." Copyright © 2021 by Jessica Lind Peterson, from *Sound Like Trapped Thunder*. Originally published in *Passages North*.

Reprinted by permission of Seneca Review Books.

"Words First Seen in Print." Copyright © 2021 by Krys Malcolm Belc, from *The Natural Mother of the Child*. Reprinted by permission of Counterpoint Press.

"Fragments, Never Sent." Copyright © 2020 by Molly McCully Brown, from *Places I've Taken My Body*. Reprinted by permission of Persea Books and Faber & Faber.

Further Reading

Below is a bibliography of works that inspired us as editors while compiling *The Lyric Essay as Resistance*. While this is by no means an exhaustive list, we hope these resources offer readers, especially teachers and students, a means of discovering more about the ways the lyric essay and resistance intersect.

—Zoë & Erica

Essays and Discussions Centering the Lyric Essay

Babbitt, Geoffrey. "On Categories & *Seneca Review*'s Book Prize." *Essay Daily*. 28 July 2017.

Bossiere, Zoë, and Erica Trabold. "In Praise of Ambiguity: The Lyric Essay in 2019." *Essay Daily*. 4 March 2019.

Boully, Jenny. "On the EEO Genre Sheet." *Betwixt and Between: Essays on the Writing Life*. Coffee House Press, 2018.

Cheng, Jennifer S., April Freely, Shamala Gallagher, Aisha Sabatini Sloan, and Addie Tsai. "The Lyric Essay's Ghosts and Shadows: A Conversation." *Essay Daily*. 12 March 2018.

Coles, Katharine. "If a Body." *Assay: A Journal of Nonfiction Studies* 5, no 2, 2019.

D'Agata, John, and Deborah Tall. "The Lyric Essay." *Seneca Review*, 1997.

Eleftheriou, Joanna. "Is Genre Ever New? Theorizing the Lyric Essay in

Its Historical Context." *Assay: A Journal of Nonfiction Studies* 4, no 1 (2017).

Noble, Billings Randon. "Consider the Platypus: Four Forms—Maybe—of the Lyric Essay." *Brevity: A Journal of Concise Literary Nonfiction.* 21 May 2022.

Norris, Maddie. "A Conversation with Elissa Washuta and Theresa Warburton." *Essay Daily.* 8 July 2019.

Ostraff, Zachary. "The Lyric Essay as a Form of Counterpoetics." *Assay: A Journal of Nonfiction Studies* 7, no 2 (2021).

Soriano, Jen. "Multiplicity from the Margins: The Expansive Truth of Intersectional Form." *Assay: A Journal of Nonfiction Studies* 5, no 1 (2018).

Wade, Julie Marie. "What's Missing Here? A Fragmentary, Lyric Essay about Fragmentary, Lyric Essays." *Literary Hub.* 28 October 2021.

Wanzer, Lyzette. "Finding a Way In: Teaching the Lyric Essay." *Essay Daily.* 5 December 2018

Waring, Kathryn. "The Case for Lyric Journalism." *Essay Daily.* 20 January 2020.

Wilson, Diana. "Laces in the Corset: Structures of Poetry and Prose That Bind the Lyric Essay." *Assay: A Journal of Nonfiction Studies* 1, no 2 (2015).

Collections and Anthologies Featuring the Lyric Essay

Adrian, Kim, ed. *The Shell Game: Writers Play with Borrowed Forms.* University of Nebraska Press, 2018.

Billings Noble, Randon, ed. *A Harp in the Stars: An Anthology of Lyric Essays.* University of Nebraska Press, 2021.

D'Agata, John, ed. *The Next American Essay.* Graywolf Press, 2003.

D'Agata, John, ed. *We Might As Well Call It the Lyric Essay.* Hobart and William Smith Colleges Press, 2015.

Green, Sarah, ed. *Welcome to the Neighborhood: An Anthology of American Coexistence.* Swallow Press, 2019.

Hollars, B. J., ed. *Blurring the Boundaries: Explorations to the Fringes of Nonfiction.* University of Nebraska Press, 2013.

Monson, Ander, and Craig Reinbold, eds. *How We Speak to One Another*. Coffee House Press, 2017.

Singer, Margot, and Nicole Walker, eds. *Bending Genre: Essays on Creative Nonfiction*. Bloomsbury, 2013.

St. Germain, Sheryl, and Margaret L. Whitford, eds. *Between Song and Story: Essays for the Twenty-First Century*. Autumn House Press, 2011.

Washuta, Elissa, and Theresa Warburton, eds. *Shapes of Native Nonfiction: Collected Essays by Contemporary Writers*. University of Washington Press, 2019.

Works on Resistance

Adsit, Janelle. *Towards a More Inclusive Creative Writing: Threshold Concepts to Guide the Literary Writing Curriculum*. Bloomsbury, 2021.

Aldrich, Marcia, ed. *Waveform: Twenty-First-Century Essays by Women*. University of Georgia Press, 2016.

Anzaldúa, Gloria. *Borderlands: The New Mestiza*. Aunt Lute Books, 2007.

Chavez, Felicia Rose. *The Anti-Racist Writing Workshop: How to Decolonize the Creative Classroom*. Haymarket Books, 2021.

Dancyger, Lilly, ed. *Burn It Down: Women Writing about Anger*. Seal Press, 2019.

Febos, Melissa. *Body Work: The Radical Power of Personal Narrative*. Catapult, 2022.

hooks, bell. "Marginality as a Site of Resistance." *Out There: Marginalization and Contemporary Culture*. Russell Ferguson and Trinh T. Minh-ha, eds. MIT Press, 1990.

Masih, Tara, ed. *The Chalk Circle: Intercultural Prizewinning Essays*. Wyatt-Mackenzie, 2012.

Mura, David. *A Stranger's Journey: Race, Identity, and Narrative Craft in Writing*. University of Georgia Press, 2018.

Yuknavitch, Lidia. *The Misfit's Manifesto*. Simon & Schuster, 2017.

Books by *The Lyric Essay as Resistance* Contributors

Belc, Krys Malcolm. *In Transit*. The Cupboard Pamphlet, 2018.

Belc, Krys Malcolm. *The Natural Mother of the Child*. Counterpoint Press, 2021.

Bertram, Lillian-Yvonne. *Personal Science*. Tupelo Press, 2017.

Bertram, Lillian-Yvonne. *Travesty Generator*. Noemi Press, 2019.

Biondolillo, Chelsea. *#Lovesong*. Etchings Press, 2016.

Biondolillo, Chelsea. *The Skinned Bird: Essays*. KERNPUNKT, 2019.

Bossiere, Zoë, and Dinty W. Moore, eds. *The Best of Brevity: Twenty Groundbreaking Years of Flash Nonfiction*. Rose Metal Press, 2020.

Boully, Jenny. *Betwixt-and-Between: Essays on the Writing Life*. Coffee House Press, 2018.

Boully, Jenny. *The Body: An Essay*. Essay Press, 2002.

Cheng, Jennifer S. *Invocation: An Essay*. New Michigan Press, 2011.

Cheng, Jennifer S. *MOON: Letters, Maps, Poems*. Tarpaulin Sky, 2018.

Febos, Melissa. *Abandon Me: Memoirs*. Bloomsbury, 2017.

Febos, Melissa. *Girlhood*. Bloomsbury, 2021.

Garcia Roberts, Chloe. *The Reveal*. Noemi Press, 2015.

Geller, Danielle. *Dog Flowers: A Memoir, An Archive*. One World, 2021.

Grass, Camellia-Berry. *Hall of Waters*. Operating System Kin(d)* Texts and Projects, 2019.

McCully Brown, Molly. *Places I've Taken My Body: Essays*. Persea Books, 2020.

McCully Brown, Molly, and Susannah Nevison. *In the Field between Us: Poems*. Persea Books, 2020.

Myint, Thirii Myo Kyaw. *The End of Peril, the End of Enmity, the End of Strife, a Haven*. Noemi Press, 2018.

Myint, Thirii Myo Kyaw. *Names for Light: A Family History*. Graywolf Press, 2021.

Peters, Torrey. *Detransition, Baby: A Novel*. Random House, 2021.

Peters, Torrey. *Infect Your Friends and Loved Ones*. Random House, 2023.

Peterson, Jessica Lind. *Sound Like Trapped Thunder*. Seneca Review Books, 2021.

Sloan, Aisha Sabatini. *Borealis (Spatial Species): An Essay*. Coffee House Press, 2021.

Sloan, Aisha Sabatini. *Dreaming of Ramadi in Detroit: Essays*. 1913 Press, 2017.

Torres, Michael. *An Incomplete List of Names*. Beacon Press, 2020.

Trabold, Erica. *Dots*. Ghost Proposal, 2021.

Trabold, Erica. *Five Plots*. Seneca Review Books, 2018.

Walters, Wendy S. *Multiply/Divide: On the American Real and Surreal*. Sarabande Books, 2015.

Walters, Wendy S. *Troy, Michigan*. Futurepoem, 2016.

Wanzer, Lyzette, ed. *Trauma, Tresses, & Truth: Untangling Our Hair Through Personal Narratives*. Lawrence Hill Books, 2022.

Washuta, Elissa. *My Body Is a Book of Rules*. Red Hen Press, 2014.

Washuta, Elissa. *White Magic*. Tin House Books, 2021.

Wilkinson, Crystal. *The Birds of Opulence*. University Press of Kentucky, 2016.

Wilkinson, Crystal. *Perfect Black*. University Press of Kentucky, 2021.

Contributors

Aisha Sabatini Sloan is the author of the essay collections *The Fluency of Light* and *Dreaming of Ramadi in Detroit*, the book-length essay *Borealis*, and, with her father, *Captioning the Archives: A Conversation in Photographs and Text*. She is an assistant professor of English and creative writing at the University of Michigan.

Camellia-Berry Grass was born and raised in rural Missouri. She is the author of *Hall of Waters* and *Let the White Dove Sing*. Her essays and poems appear in *The Texas Review*, *Waxwing*, *DIAGRAM*, and *Barrelhouse*, among other publications. In 2019 she was a finalist for the Krause Essay Prize. She currently lives in Philadelphia, where she teaches in the MFA program in creative writing at Rosemont College.

Chelsea Biondolillo is a collage artist and the author of *The Skinned Bird* and two prose chapbooks, *Ologies* and *#Lovesong*. Her essays have appeared in *Best American Science* and *Nature Writing 2016*, *Orion*, *Guernica*, *River Teeth*, *DIAGRAM*, *Brevity*, and elsewhere. Her collages have been shown in Oregon and Washington, and anthologized in *Transitional Moments*, by *Kolaj Magazine*. She lives in a small town, between a mountain and a river, just south of Portland, Oregon.

Chloe Garcia Roberts is a poet and translator from Spanish and Chinese. She is the author of a book of poetry, *The Reveal*, and her translations include Li Shangyin's *Derangements of My Contemporaries* and the collected poems of Li Shangyin. Her essays, poems, and translations have appeared in *BOMB*, *A Public Space*, *Kenyon Review*, and *Yale Review* among others. She lives outside Boston and works as deputy editor of *Harvard Review*.

Crystal Wilkinson, Kentucky's Poet Laureate, is the award-winning author of *Perfect Black*, and three works of fiction. She is the recipient of an NAACP Image Award, an O. Henry Prize, and an Ernest Gaines Prize. *Praise Song for the Kitchen Ghosts*, a culinary memoir, is forthcoming from Clarkson Potter/Penguin Random House.

Danielle Geller's first book, *Dog Flowers*, was published by One World/Random House in 2021. Her work has appeared in *Guernica*, *The New Yorker*, and *Brevity*. She teaches at the University of Victoria and is a faculty mentor for the low-rez MFA program at the Institute of American Indian Arts. She is a citizen of the Navajo Nation: born to the Tsi'naajinii, born for the bilagaana.

Elissa Washuta is a member of the Cowlitz Indian Tribe and the author of *White Magic*, *Starvation Mode*, and *My Body Is a Book of Rules*. With Theresa Warburton, she co-edited the anthology *Shapes of Native Nonfiction: Collected Essays by Contemporary Writers*. Elissa is an associate professor at The Ohio State University, where she teaches in the MFA Program in Creative Writing.

Hea-Ream Lee is a writer and teacher from the East Coast living in the desert. She received an MFA in creative nonfiction at the University of Arizona, where she edited fiction for *Sonora Review* and currently teaches undergraduate writing. Hea-Ream's work appears in *Shenandoah*, *Terrain.org*, *Populla*, *Hobart*, and others, and she has received fellowships from the Wormfarm Institute and the Bread Loaf Environmental Writers' Conference. She is working on a book about seed banks and longing.

Jennifer S. Cheng is the author of *MOON: Letters, Maps, Poems*, named a Publishers Weekly "Best Book of 2018"; *House A*, selected by Claudia Rankine for the Omnidawn Poetry Book Prize; and *Invocation: An Essay*, an image-text chapbook. She has received fellowships and awards from Brown University, the University of Iowa, the National Endowment for the Arts, the U.S. Fulbright program, Kundiman, MacDowell, Bread Loaf, and the Academy of American Poets. *www.jenniferscheng.com*

Jenny Boully is a Guggenheim fellow in general nonfiction. She is the author of *Betwixt-and-Between: Essays on the Writing Life*. Her previous books include not merely because of the unknown that was stalking toward them, *The Book of Beginnings and Endings: Essays, [one love affair]*, *of the mismatched teacups, of the single-serving spoon: a book of failures*, and *The Body: An Essay*. She teaches at Bennington College.

Jessica Lind Peterson is an essayist, playwright, and theater artist. Her essays have appeared in *Orion, Seneca Review, River Teeth, Passages North, Alaska Quarterly Review*, and others. Her first collection, *Sound Like Trapped Thunder*, was awarded the 2020 Deborah Tall Lyric Essay Book Prize and was a finalist for a Minnesota Book Award. She lives with her family in Duluth, Minnesota.

Krys Malcolm Belc is the author of the flash nonfiction chapbook *In Transit* and the memoir *The Natural Mother of the Child*. He lives in Philadelphia with his partner and their three young children.

Lillian-Yvonne Bertram is the author of *Travesty Generator*, longlisted for the 2020 National Book Award for Poetry. Their other poetry books include the chapbook *How Narrow My Escapes, Personal Science, a slice from the cake made of air*, and *But a Storm Is Blowing from Paradise*. Their fifth book, *Negative Money*, is forthcoming from Soft Skull Press in 2023.

213

Lyzette Wanzer's work appears in over thirty literary journals, books, and magazines. Her research interests include professional development for creative writers, the lyrical essay form, Black feminism, and critical race theory. Her book *Trauma, Tresses & Truth: Untangling Our Hair through Personal Narratives*, examines the policing, perception, and persecution of African American and Afro Latina women's natural hair.

Melissa Febos is the best-selling author of four books, most recently, *Girlhood*, winner of the National Book Critics Circle Award in criticism, and *Body Work: The Radical Power of Personal Narrative*. She is the recipient of awards and fellowships from the Guggenheim Foundation, the National Endowment for the Arts, MacDowell, LAMBDA Literary, the Barbara Deming Foundation, the Black Mountain Institute, the British Library, and others. She is an associate professor at the University of Iowa.

Michael Torres was born and brought up in Pomona, California. His first collection, *An Incomplete List of Names*, was a National Poetry Series selection. Visit him at: *michaeltorreswriter.com*.

Molly McCully Brown is the author of the essay collection *Places I've Taken My Body* and the poetry collection *The Virginia State Colony for Epileptics and Feebleminded*, which won the 2016 Lexi Rudnitsky First Book Prize and was named a New York Times Critics' Top Book of 2017. With Susannah Nevison, she is also the coauthor of the poetry collection *In The Field Between Us*. She teaches at Old Dominion University, where she is an assistant professor of English and creative nonfiction and a member of the MFA core faculty.

Thirii Myo Kyaw Myint is the author of the novel *The End of Peril, the End of Enmity, the End of Strife, a Haven*, which won an Asian/Pacific American Award for Literature, and *Names for Light: A Family History*, which won the Graywolf Press Nonfiction Prize, and was a finalist for the PEN Open Book Award. She is an assistant professor of English at Amherst College.

Torrey Peters is the author of the novel *Detransition, Baby*, published by One World, which won the 2021 PEN/Hemingway award for debut fiction. It was also a finalist for the National Book Critics Circle Award and was longlisted for the Women's Prize for Fiction. A collection of four novellas, titled *Infect Your Friends and Loved Ones*, will be published by Random House in 2023.

Wendy S. Walters is concentration head in nonfiction and associate professor in the writing program of the School of the Arts at Columbia University, New York. She is the author or editor of four books, including *Multiply/Divide: On the American Real and Surreal*. She is completing her next book, an argument against the use of white paint.

About the Editors

Zoë Bossiere is a genderfluid writer from Tucson, Arizona. She received her doctorate in creative nonfiction and in rhetoric and composition from Ohio University. She is the managing editor of *Brevity: A Journal of Concise Literary Nonfiction* and coeditor of its anthology, *The Best of Brevity*. She also hosts a podcast interviewing nonfiction writers about their debut books for the New Book Network's New Books in Literature channel.

Erica Trabold is the author of *Five Plots*, winner of the inaugural Deborah Tall Lyric Essay Book Prize. Her lyric essays appear in *Brevity*, *The Rumpus*, *Passages North*, *The Collagist*, *South Dakota Review*, and *Seneca Review*. She received her master of fine arts from Oregon State University. Erica currently writes and teaches in central Virginia, where she is an assistant professor at Sweet Briar College.